This book belongs to...

_____

a woman joyfully committed to
praying for her husband

ELIZABETH GEORGE

15 Verses TO PRAY FOR Your Husband

HARVEST HOUSE PUBLISHERS
EUGENE, OREGON

Cover by Dugan Design Group, Bloomington, Minnesota

15 VERSES TO PRAY FOR YOUR HUSBAND
Copyright © 2015 Elizabeth George
Published by Harvest House Publishers
Eugene, Oregon 97402
www.harvesthousepublishers.com

Library of Congress Cataloging-in-Publication Data
George, Elizabeth, 1944-
15 verses to pray for your husband / Elizabeth George.
    pages cm
Includes bibliographical references.
ISBN 978-0-7369-2677-5 (pbk.)
ISBN 978-0-7369-4493-9 (eBook)
1. Husbands—Prayers and devotions. 2. Marriage—Religious aspects—Christianity. I. Title.
II. Title: Fifteen verses to pray for your husband.
BV283.H8G38 2015
242'.8435—dc23
                                                    2015010135

Printed in the United States of America

16 17 18 19 20 21 22 23 / BP-JH / 10 9 8 7 6 5 4 3 2

Contents

Answering God's Call to Pray

Lord, teach us to pray...
LUKE 11:1

On any journey, like that of becoming a faithful prayer warrior for your husband, a first step must always be taken. I remember when I took my first step toward seriously learning how to pray. It was on Mother's Day, May 8, 1983. My daughter Katherine (age 13) gave me the gift of a tiny wordless book. It was purple (Kath's favorite color)...and I still have it because it's a real keepsake to me. One reason it's so special is because my precious daughter gave it to me!

Katherine came up with the idea for the gift and arranged with Jim (my husband and Kath's dad) to do extra chores so she could earn the money to purchase something for me for Mother's Day. Then the two of them went off together to shop for just the right present for Mom. The little treasure was then inscribed by Katherine on the bookplate in her careful handwriting, lovingly gift-wrapped, and proudly given to me on that Sunday morning so many years ago.

Oh, believe me, I screamed! I squealed! I did everything but turn cartwheels to express my thanks to my sweet daughter. But then I faced a problem—what to do with a wordless book? For several months I let the small book lie on the coffee table so my dear Katherine would know how much I truly appreciated it. Then one day, not knowing exactly what to do with it, I moved it into the bookcase...and it was gone...

...until September 12, four months later. That day was my tenth birthday in the Lord. As I sat alone before God, I looked back over my first ten years as God's child. Of course, that led to a time of thanking Him for His mercy, His grace, His care, His guidance, His wisdom, my salvation through Christ, and so much more.

On and on my prayers of appreciation to God gushed. Then after dabbing my eyes with a tissue, I turned my thoughts forward and I prayed, "Lord, as I start a new decade with You, is there anything missing from my Christian life?"

Oh, dear friend, I can only report to you that before I put the question mark on the question, I knew in my heart what the answer was: prayer. God was calling me to pray. To make prayer a priority. To pay serious attention to prayer. To become a woman of prayer.

And just as suddenly, I knew what to do with that tiny purple wordless book. I ran to the bookcase and pulled out that little treasure. "There you are!" I cried, acknowledging that it had been waiting for four months for that very day and this very use. Thrilled, I opened it up and wrote on the very first page:

> I dedicate and purpose to spend the next ten years in the Lord, Lord willing, developing a meaningful prayer life.

Making a Commitment

Why did I pick ten years for my commitment to develop a meaningful prayer life? Probably because it was my tenth birthday in Christ. Today, as I am telling this story, those ten years have come and gone. And I want to tell you right now—I am still learning how to pray!

As you probably already know, you and I won't ever wake up one day at a point where we can mark "Learn to pray" off of our to-do list. No, no one prays enough. And no one prays as passionately as she would like to pray or should pray. And no one prays for as many people as need to be prayed for.

And so we must continue on our journey into prayer until we "get it," until we can say that we've begun to know even a little bit about prayer. And until that happens, a lot of Christians pray what I call "Christopher Robin" prayers. He's the boy in A.A. Milne's classic book *When We Were Very Young*. Little Christopher Robin struggled with his evening "vespers."[1] He became so distracted by anything and everything—you name it—that he couldn't remember who or what to pray for. So he ended up praying "God bless_____" prayers, filling in the blank with the names of family members and friends, his nanny and pets...until he got distracted all over again.

I can relate to Christopher Robin's "prayer" experience. And maybe you can too. That's exactly how I prayed...up until I made my commitment to answer God's call to pray. Like Christopher Robin, my mind wandered. I didn't know who to pray for, or how to pray for them. So my prayers basically consisted of lame efforts, until they finally wound down to a muttered "God bless me and my family today."

Getting Organized—Taking a Step

And so I started writing out prayer requests in that little purple book. But it became apparent very quickly that I was going to run out of blank pages—they measured only 3 x 5 inches each! Can you imagine trying to fit in every area of your life, all the people you know, all the decisions you need to make, and all the commitments, goals, and resolutions for spiritual growth and change in a miniature journal?

I realized if I was going to be a faithful prayer warrior, I was going to have to do something. So I went to our bookcase and grabbed an empty three-ring binder, and then searched for some lined notebook paper. I had prayed enough days using that sweet little book to realize I wanted to pray through the areas and issues in my daily life in priority order.

Next task? To create a tab for each section of my new prayer notebook. My first tab was "God" for my relationship with Him. My next most-important priority was my husband, who received my next tab—"Jim"—and a bunch of lined pages. From that day onward, Jim received my almost-daily prayers for his upcoming day as well as anything and everything he was experiencing or would be facing in the future.

Maybe you can guess the progression of my tabs in that battered binder that would change my prayer life—and my life! "Katherine" and "Courtney" each got a tab. So did my "Home." Next I created the tab "Self" for my prayer needs for growth and goals for improvement. And "Ministry" completed my initial setup.

Back then I didn't have this book you are reading, but knowing now what I experienced with my Jim and his life, and as I talk to and read letters and emails from wives around the world, I urge you to set up some kind of system for prayer. It can be a notebook or a journal, a phone app or a personal file you create on your computer.

Whatever you do, try to incorporate the 15 areas of your husband's life that are presented in this book. You can start right now—today—by deciding to make a new page for your husband as you read each chapter. Whether you want to pray all of the prayers in this book each day, or focus on just one each day, use the prayer provided there to pray for your husband.

Praying for Your Husband

Hopefully you've already had your husband as a key focal point of your prayers up to now. If so, your husband is a blessed man to have you as his wife! To make him your special "prayer project" for life, here are a few suggestions and even cautions to keep in mind.

Pray without expecting instant results. God is always at work. As the psalmist wrote, "He who keeps you will not slumber. Behold, He who keeps Israel shall neither slumber nor sleep" (Psalm 121:3-4).

God doesn't work according to your timetable. I'm sure you know this from firsthand experience. For instance, God has been patient with you so far, hasn't He? And yet He has been at work in your life. You're not where you need to be or where you're going to be, but you also aren't where you used to be!

Now you must apply this knowledge of God to your husband. And so you pray faithfully and forever for your husband. That's your commitment of love. And, as you pray for your husband, don't expect or look for any overnight miracles. Learn a lesson from Monica, the mother of Augustine, one of the early church fathers. This devout believer and devoted mother prayed for decades before God opened her son's heart and he embraced Christ at age 31.

First Corinthians 13 tells us that "love suffers long...[and] bears all things, believes all things, hopes all things, endures all things" (verses 4 and 7). That, my praying sister-in-Christ, is to be our approach to praying for our husbands. We pray no matter what. We pray—and suffer long, patient while we bear and endure all things, always believing and never losing hope.

Don't get discouraged in the course of your prayer journey. It's exactly that—a journey! That means it involves time and takes time, even a lifetime. Be persistent yet patient as you pray. God's "ears are open" to your prayers and your cries; He sees you in secret, and acts when and how He chooses (1 Peter 3:12; Matthew 6:6).

Pray, even when you don't feel like it. When you are discouraged or frustrated with what is or isn't happening in your marriage, pray! God knows your heart, your dreams and desires, and your sorrows. Begin your time of prayer telling your heavenly Father all about what is and isn't happening in your marriage, your home, and your life—and your husband's too.

But also do as the writer of Psalm 77 did. For ten verses, Asaph lamented to God about his grim situation. Then he had a "Wait a minute!" wake-up call, and acknowledged, "'This is my anguish; but I will remember the years at the right hand of the Most High.' I will remember the works of the LORD; surely I will remember Your wonders of old" (verses 10-11).

Asaph turned a corner in his thoughts and changed his thinking pattern. He resolutely stated "but I will" and then praised God and affirmed that God is, has been, and always will be faithful and good, never wrong in what He is doing.

Pray, expecting to do battle. All through the entire chapter of John 17 we see Jesus, the Son of God, in prayer to His Father in heaven. In what is often called Jesus' high-priestly prayer, you will learn that the world is a battleground in which the forces of evil are at war with those under God's loving authority. Satan and the evil system he has established are constantly attacking God's people. With that in mind, Jesus prayed in John 17 for His 12 disciples, and by extension, He prayed for all His followers, including you and your husband.

What did Jesus pray for? That the Father would keep all believers for all time, including you and your husband, safe from Satan's power and keep you set apart, holy, and pure. Hopefully your husband is praying for you, but even if he isn't, you must embrace your role as a prayer warrior. It's vital that you see yourself as a soldier doing battle when you pray for your beloved husband. Isn't it encouraging to know that Jesus is in heaven also interceding on your husband's behalf? What a team!

Pray, knowing the Holy Spirit is interceding as well. Sometimes we as wives don't know how to pray for our husbands. If you are even a little like me, you are so close to your husband's struggles that you are often frozen in fear or bewilderment. It is during these times of desperation that you and I can count on the Holy Spirit along with God, the Father, and Jesus, His Son. When you don't know what to think or how to pray for your husband, you can know that the Holy Spirit knows, and is making intercession on his behalf.

Romans 8:26 says, "The Spirit...helps in our weaknesses. For we do not know what we should pray for as we ought, but the Spirit Himself makes intercession for us with groanings which cannot be uttered." We know we are in good hands because the next verse says that such intervention is always in harmony with God's will: "He makes intercession for the saints according to the will of God" (verse 27). Be encouraged as you pray that it is not only you praying, but Jesus is interceding at the right hand of the Father, and the Spirit is involved as well. The whole Trinity is joining you in prayers for your husband!

Pray, leaving the results to God. God tells His people to pray without ceasing (1 Thessalonians 5:17). And so you do as He asks and pray! But the real comfort in praying for your husband is leaving your requests in God's lap, so to speak. Yes, you pray. And yes, you watch and wait for results. And yes, you may pray and watch and wait for decades. But each day—and every time you experience even a hint of anxiety or frustration—you lay your concerns into God's hands to do *as He wills* and *when He wills.* Philippians 4:6 tells you to "let your requests be made known to God." And afterward? You experience "the peace of God" (verse 7).

Focus on Your Blessings

In one of his many psalms, David gave us some practical instruction when he wrote, "Bless the LORD, O my soul, and forget not all His benefits" (Psalm 103:2). When you are praying and storming the gates of heaven on behalf of your husband, it's easy to focus on what you don't have, or on what it doesn't seem like God is doing. It's easy to question God and start asking Him, "Why isn't anything changing? Why aren't You fixing this? Why aren't You answering my prayers? What am I doing wrong?" But in the midst of all our asking, David nudges us to remember and notice all of God's blessings, all His "benefits."

A true confession—I love Psalm 103:2 and took seriously its exhortation to "forget not" the many ways God blesses me. So on Day One of using my little purple wordless book for prayer, I set up a page entitled "Blessings" and dove in to list all of the blessings that had occurred in my day—and it was only 10:00 a.m.

What was I thinking? Can you imagine—a single page for

tracking *all* of God's blessings to you as His child, especially on a 3 x 5-inch page? Within minutes that page was full, and I wasn't even finished! Jesus' words leapt into my mind: "How much more will your Father who is in heaven give good things to those who ask Him" (Matthew 7:11). Oh, does He ever!

Needless to say, when I made my large loose-leaf notebook, I created an individual tab marked "Blessings" to make a record of the multitude of ways God was blessing and encouraging me. (And in no time at all, page after page became filled with evidence of God's blessings, to the point of filling up a file folder in our file cabinet.)

Don't forget each day—and multiple times during your day— to at least acknowledge God's blessings. Keeping a record of His benefits makes you ultra-aware of God's presence in your days, hours, and minutes. Then when you run up against an exceptionally down day and you are especially discouraged, maybe even depressed, pull your lists out, review them, and praise God for His past blessings. Your spirit will be revived.

Looking Forward

Prayer is truly the queen of all the habits you could desire as a woman of faith. As you make your way through this book and discover the different ways you can be praying for your husband, I want you to take this thought with you:

> He who has learned how to pray
> has learned the greatest secret
> of a holy and a happy life.[2]

I'm sure you caught the word *learned*. All of your learning and efforts in prayer will help lead you to "a holy and happy life." And the beautiful miracle is that a holy and a happy life can be yours each day...every day...as you answer God's call to pray. So let the outpouring of your heart for your husband begin now—today! The opportunity and privilege of talking to God through prayer is yours.

As you step into deepening your prayer life and praying for your husband, you will be placing his name in 15 prayers to pray for him. But before you launch your prayer project for your husband, there's one place I hope you will write *your* name. The declaration that follows was made by George Müller. This man was a persistent, relentless pray-er. Without asking a single person for help or even sharing about his needs, he prayed to God to provide daily for the many orphaned children he took in. Through fervent prayer, he was able to care for all the needs— food, clothing, health, and education—of more than 10,000 children during his lifetime.

Wouldn't you like to have Müller's unrelenting faith and the same kinds of answers to your prayers for your husband? You can! Especially if you develop George Müller's degree of resolve as your pray for your husband:

> I live in the spirit of prayer. I pray as I walk about, when I lie down and when I rise up. And the answers are always coming. Thousand and tens of thousands of times have my prayers been answered. When once I am persuaded that a thing is right and for the glory of God, I go on praying for it until the answer comes. George Müller never gives up![3]

_____ never gives up!

(Your name here)

Chapter 1

Praying for Your Husband's Spiritual Growth

We also...do not cease to pray for you, and to ask
that you may be filled with the knowledge of His
will in all wisdom and spiritual understanding;
that you may walk worthy of the Lord, fully
pleasing Him, being fruitful in every good work and
increasing in the knowledge of God; strengthened
with all might, according to His glorious power,
for all patience and longsuffering with joy.

COLOSSIANS 1:9-11

Every marriage has its beginning. For Jim and me, that beginning was on the campus of the University of Oklahoma. With my new fall schedule, my path to my ballet class brought me face-to-face every Monday, Wednesday, and Friday with a very cute and friendly guy. To this day I'm so glad I enrolled in that ballet class to fulfill my need for fine arts credits.

The very cute and friendly guy was known on the campus as

Smilin' Jim George, which fit perfectly as he smiled and laughed and greeted everyone on his way—which included me. Three times a week we were smiling and saying "Hi" to each other. Then a friend of Jim's arranged a blind date for us—and we were married eight months later! He, the scientist and pharmacy major, married the ballerina-English major. What a match...or was it a mismatch?

More of our story will come a little later, but let me just say that Jim and I spent the next five years basically doing everything wrong in our marriage. Then we added two little girls to the mix and spent another three years floundering and doing everything wrong as parents. You see, we had no foundation, no guidelines, no principles to show us the way to a happy, fulfilling marriage and family.

But miracle of miracles and by God's grace, we became a Christian couple! (Thank You, Lord!) That's when we began to grow in Christ. And on Day One at church we realized when the pastor said, "Turn in your Bibles to..." that we needed two Bibles pronto. Easy enough! We took care of that need immediately after the church service and purchased matching Bibles.

And best of all, we began reading our Bibles the very next day. The next Sunday we joined a class for young marrieds. During our class we also signed up for a Friday night couples' Bible study. We were sponges! Everything that came along, we got on board. We also began memorizing Scripture. And we enrolled in an evening Bible class at a local Bible institute.

After being in the world for so long, we were hungry—starving!—for something of substance, for something meaningful, for something that gave us answers to our many questions, such as, What is the purpose of our lives? How could we have a meaningful marriage? Where could we get help with raising our two toddlers?

If you have read any of the books Jim and I have written, you may have been tempted to think, *Wow, what a wonderful life Jim and Elizabeth have.* Well, let me quickly tell you that it wasn't that way in the beginning. After eight years of marriage and three of those years as parents, we were soooo lost and confused—and miserable! For almost a decade we had little or no peace in our home. Arguments abounded. We disagreed on just about everything.

Once thing led to another until we were truly each going our own way. Jim was deeply consumed with his job as a pharmaceutical salesman. And I was attending classes day and night to earn a master's degree and obtain a license in marriage and family counseling. (Can you hear me laughing? I think I hear you laughing!) We each admit we entertained thoughts of divorce. We were the proverbial flailing couple who was going down for the third time...and taking two little girls with us.

And along came Jesus. How we loved and embraced the good news of the gospel! With Jesus came new life. We were new creatures in Christ. Old things passed away. Behold, all things became new! We were stunned by the truths of the new birth and the complete forgiveness of our past and sins. Our minds reeled from the knowledge that our slates of sins were wiped clean by Jesus' death. In Christ, we had a second chance. A new beginning.

As we grew spiritually, we learned about the presence of the Holy Spirit in us—and every believer. We tasted firsthand the amazing transformation that occurs as followers of Jesus feed on the Word of God and commit to obeying what the Bible reveals about the behaviors God desires in His people. We still failed often...but we were definitely growing.

These same experiences are available to you too—and to your husband—as you commit to following Christ and growing spiritually mature. So while you are growing in the Lord, you can—and should—pray for your husband's spiritual growth. Here are two scenarios to consider in your marriage and as you pray.

What If My Husband Is Not a Christian?

If your husband is not a Christian, then your first and foremost assignment is to pray daily for God to draw your beloved to Himself. I cannot urge you strongly enough to pray faithfully. It is entirely possible that you are the only person on the face of the earth praying for him. That means if you don't pray for him, then probably no one is! The Bible says, "The effective, fervent prayer of a righteous man avails much" (James 5:16). And the same is true of the effective, fervent prayer of a righteous *wife*. It avails and accomplishes much! Your assignment from God is to pray, to keep on praying no matter what, and to trust God.

And while you are praying for your husband, pray for God to send people to share their faith with him. Pray for someone to give him a book that shows him the way to Christ. That's how Jim and I became a Christian couple. One of the doctors Jim called on each month was a vibrant Christian, and he gave Jim a copy of a Christian book. (And, by the way, this doctor purchased this one book title by the hundreds and gave one to every person who entered his offices!) Well, Jim read the book for all the wrong reasons—he read it so *if* the doctor asked him about the book on his next sales visit, Jim could smile and say yes, he had read it and then politely and knowledgeably discuss it.

Who knew that book would turn Jim's world upside down?! Like the apostle Paul in Philippians 3, God "apprehended" or laid hold upon Jim through the scriptures and truths presented in that book.

Well, as with all good things, Jim wanted to share it with his spouse—that's me! Immediately he asked me to read the book. In all honesty I told him, "Of course I'll read it." After all, reading books for my studies and papers was about all I did (and my messy house was proof of that!). Unfortunately that book ended up getting lost in my bookcase for the next two years. And, like Jim, the day I picked it up and began reading it was the day my life changed forever. Suddenly God turned my life upside-down too—and we became a couple after God's own heart. That's when we wholeheartedly and in perfect unity jumped into the race that is set before us (Hebrews 12:1).

I cannot encourage you enough to pray for your unbelieving husband. God can turn your husband upside-down and inside-out. God is able to break through the hardest of hearts. He delights in showing people the way to know Him and experience His love and forgiveness. And prayer is your direct avenue to God. Each prayer you utter is from your heart to His. Praying for your husband is your supreme act of love. As a famous theologian noted, "There is nothing that makes us love a man so much as praying for him."[1]

What If My Husband Is a Christian?

If your husband is a believer, then don't forget to pray for God to move him to *want* to grow as a Christian.

Maybe this is a good time for us to remind ourselves that we are not called to nag our husbands to read their Bibles and be more committed to their spiritual growth. As a mentor told me when I was still a new believer, I am not to attempt to take on the role the Holy Spirit has in prompting and convicting my husband of his need to be growing in Christ.

And it's true. As a wife, I am not responsible for my husband's spiritual growth. But I *am* responsible to grow myself and to fulfill God's commands to me to love and respect my husband, to be his helper and his number one encourager in all things.[2]

So What's a Wife to Do?

Number one on your "To-Do List for Wives" is to pray, pray, pray! Instead of unleashing or dumping your frustrations and disappointments in your husband on him, pray! Let God know all about your concerns. When you tell God the desires of your heart, and pray for something that you *know* God wants to occur in your husband's life—like grow in Christ, you are most definitely telling the right person!

And go ahead and give God the reasons you are asking for what you are praying. First on that list should be your husband's spiritual growth because that is something God wants for him. Praying in this way centers your prayers on God—not on yourself or on something that makes your life easier or better.

You can also ask God to plant within your husband's heart a desire to grow in the knowledge of God because that growth will make your husband a godly man and a better spiritual leader for you and any children you have. These are roles God lays out for all Christian husbands. To pray for this is not self-serving. No, this request also lines up with *God's will* for husbands to lead those in the home (1 Corinthians 11:3; 1 Timothy 3:5).

Here's another way you can love your husband: Pray for a spiritual mentor to take your husband under his wing. This too is a request that is biblical and pleases God. Paul had his Timothy to nurture and train. Joshua had his Moses to watch and learn from. Barnabas took his nephew John Mark and taught him everything he knew about serving God. That, dear fellow wife, is what God wants for your husband—to be mentored, and to one day mentor others.

When it comes to our prayers, God gives us these guidelines—and measuring sticks—to help us check our motives. They come from James 4:2-3:

— "You do not have because you do not ask." God's message? Make sure you are praying and asking God to work in your husband's heart.

— "You ask and do not receive, because you ask amiss, that you may spend it on your pleasures." Remember you are not asking for anything for yourself, but for what you know God wants from and for your husband.

The first of these two guidelines on prayer from James 4 tells us that just maybe the reason we aren't seeing God at work in our lives and marriages and families is because of our own neglect to pray. Therefore, we don't have what we and our spouse and children need because we haven't asked God for it. God's word to us is to start asking—and keep asking.

The second teaching warns us that once we start asking, we are to check our heart. So we start praying and asking...and maybe we are still not receiving or seeing what we're asking for. We wonder, *What's wrong?* God says it is possible that we are not receiving answers because we are asking "amiss." We are asking for the wrong things or for the wrong reasons or motives.

One study Bible helps us understand these two principles from James 4:2-3 with these words:

> Do you talk to God at all? When you do, what do you talk about? Do you ask only to satisfy your desires? Do you seek God's approval for what you already plan to do? Our prayers will become

powerful when we allow God to change our desires
so that they perfectly correspond to his will for us
(1 John 3:21,22).[3]

A Prayer to Pray

Here is a perfect prayer to pray for your husband's spiritual
growth and maturity. And yes, I can say it's perfect because it is
right out of the Bible—God's Word straight from His heart! I
have tweaked these verses to be prayed to God as your personal
prayer for your husband. Pray these verses fervently and passionately—and often!—from your heart to God's heart and put
your beloved's name in the blanks. Before you read on, read the
passage that makes up the heart of this prayer. You will find it
at the top of the first page of this chapter.

My Prayer for My Husband
Colossians 1:9-11

*Father God, I do not cease to pray for _____,
and to ask that _____ may be filled with the
knowledge of Your will in all wisdom and spiritual
understanding; that _____ may walk worthy
of You, Lord, fully pleasing You, being fruitful in every
good work and increasing in his knowledge of You,
God; that _____ may be strengthened with
all might, according to Your glorious power. Amen.*

Isn't this a great prayer?! This and every prayer in the Bible was uttered for a purpose. So let's discover the purpose and reason for this exquisite prayer we are praying for our husbands.

When the apostle Paul prayed and wrote this prayer, he was far away from people he loved in the church at Colosse. In fact, he was imprisoned in Rome, more than 1000 miles away. One day, Epaphras, the pastor of the church in Colosse, showed up to visit Paul. This faithful pastor poured out to Paul his grave concerns for the spiritual conditions in the Colossian church.

The result of this man's loving concern for the spiritual condition of his friends was the book of Colossians. With a heavy heart filled with love, Paul then wrote a "letter" to the people in the church at Colosse. In it, Paul shared God's answers and solutions to the people's problems.

As we unpack the three verses of the soaring, heartfelt prayer in Colossians 1:9-11, think about how significant the implications of this prayer are in the spiritual life of your husband.

Pray for your husband fervently and without ceasing (Colossians 1:9). Like Paul, your prayers for your partner's spiritual growth should be frequent—and forever! As Paul wrote, "We do not cease to pray." This is a good reminder for all wives that your prayers for your husband are not to be a one-time event. When your husband has an issue, need, or crisis, or you have a concern regarding him, you can offer up a quick prayer anytime and anywhere, regardless of what you are doing.

However, you cannot be satisfied with random "arrow" prayers shot up to heaven from here and there, now and then. Yes, there is a place for quickly sharing your heart with God as you go through your day and think about someone, or your heart is breaking, or you need some on-the-spot wisdom. But prayer is also doing business with God. It's sort of like preparing a presentation to share at work or to a committee or to a board.

You have some idea or change or improvement that you think would better your employer's business or will improve the work you are involved in. So you create, and edit, and change, and fine-tune, and polish a presentation to give before the powers-that-be for their consideration—and hopefully, their approval.

Your formal prayers to God are like a presentation. There is something you want desperately. You want your husband to become a Christian. Or you want your husband to desire to grow as a Christian. This is serious business—which you present to God. You pour out your heart to God and your reasons for what you are asking.

I love the picture—and prayer—presented in 2 Kings 19:14-18. When King Hezekiah received a threatening letter demanding that he surrender to an opposing army, what did he do?

> Hezekiah received the letter from the hand of the messengers, and read it; and Hezekiah went up to the house of the Lord, and spread it before the Lord. Then Hezekiah prayed before the Lord...(verses 14-15).

Hezekiah went to the temple, laid the letter before the Lord, and prayed, appealed, and presented his problem and his requests and his reasons to God.

King Hezekiah shows us how to come before God with something that is vital to us and to Him. And so does the apostle Paul. His prayers were "always" (Philippians 1:4), "without ceasing" (1 Thessalonians 5:17), and he prayed "constantly" (2 Timothy 1:3 NASB).

Now, what is it you should be praying for?

Pray that your husband will grow in the knowledge of God's will (Colossians 1:9). The focus of your prayer is that your husband "may be filled with the knowledge of His will." The Bible says that "if we ask anything according to His will, He hears us" (1 John 5:14). So praying that your husband knows and lives and acts according to God's will is extremely important.

How is your husband (and you too) to identify God's will? God's will is not a mystery that is unknowable, so what else is needed for knowing it? The next phrase in Colossians 1:9 gives you the answer: "all wisdom and spiritual understanding."

You are to pray for *wisdom* for your husband. "Wisdom" is the ability to gather and organize principles from Scripture. And you are also to pray for your husband's *spiritual understanding*—that he will understand what he reads and studies in God's Word. That's because "understanding" is the application of those principles in your husband's daily life. That is the essence of God's will!

Pray that your husband will please God (Colossians 1:10). As I said, this is a marvelous and beautiful prayer to pray—that your husband will please God! Pleasing God occurs when your husband obeys God's commands—when he does God's will. You are praying that your husband will follow and obey God by walking in a worthy manner, which will result in bearing the fruit of the Spirit in his life—the fruit of love, joy peace, patience, kindness, goodness, faithfulness, gentleness, and self-control (Galatians 5:22-23). Pleasing God also occurs when your husband grows in his knowledge of God.

Colossians 1:10 sums up how your husband can please God—in a Spirit-controlled walk, in godly actions, and in the diligent study of God's Word. And you are privileged to pray for him to do just that!

Pray that your husband will be strengthened by God (Colossians 1:11). You are probably familiar with Paul's powerful statement, "I can do all things through Christ who strengthens me" (Philippians 4:13). Similarly Paul focused on God's strength in his prayer in Colossians 1:11, that believers would be "strengthened with all might, according to His glorious power."

Let's follow the path of Paul's prayer: In prayer, you, dear praying wife, ask Christ to enable your husband with His power to be God's man. You ask God to infuse your husband with His strength to love you and his children and to lead your family unit through the pressures and adversities of daily living. And you pray fervently for your husband to be strengthened with all might, "according to His glorious power." You ask God that your husband would be made strong with God's glorious power, with God's incredible strength—so your husband can have "all patience and longsuffering with joy."

Reflecting on God's glorious power and strength, devotional Bible commentator Matthew Henry wrote:

> To be strengthened is to be furnished by the grace
> of God for every good work, and fortified by that
> grace against every evil [work]: it is to be enabled
> to do our duty, and still to hold fast our integrity.[4]

And here's the ultimate blessing of God's glorious power: When your husband is strengthened by that power, there will be only one way to explain his life and character, and that is God! And because there is no human explanation for your husband's walk and the fruit in his life, God Himself will receive all the glory. God will be glorified, which is every Christian's highest goal and purpose—"to do all to the glory of God" (1 Corinthians 10:31).

Beyond Prayer, What Can You Do?

1. *Decide to be growing spiritually yourself.* This is the most important decision you need to be making each day. Put the Lord first in your heart each day, and He will give you the wisdom to be the kind of wife your husband needs. Realize that the time you spend reading and studying God's Word and bending your soul in devoted prayer are holy times of preparation, not only for your day and your responsibilities and your walk with God, but to prepare yourself for ministry to your husband and family and to others. The spiritual impact you have on your husband and children will be in direct proportion to the time you spend away from people and with God in a daily quiet time of preparation.

2. *Accept the life God has given you.* Every woman has dreams of how perfect their marriage will be. But sadly, real life doesn't always turn out as desired. Maybe your dreams are all coming true. If so, be thankful—extremely thankful!—and pray for your husband's continued growth and maturity. Or maybe you are waiting for something positive to happen in your husband and your marriage. Life has a way of putting up detours, roadblocks, and immovable barriers in your path. But rather than having a pity party or giving in to anger or giving up in hopelessness, chose to always give thanks. I know this is the opposite of what you are feeling and thinking, but it is God's prescription for maintaining Christlike behavior. It is God's will: "In everything give thanks; for this is the will of God in Christ Jesus for you" (1 Thessalonians 5.18). "Everything" means exactly that. Everything even includes the way your husband does or does not respond to God. Remember, *your* job is to love your husband

and to pray to God to change his heart. *God's* job is to do the changing—in His time and in His way.

3. *Acknowledge the sufficiency of God.* Problems and disappointment are means God uses to give you opportunities to live out His will even though life isn't going exactly the way you had hoped. God is always at work in you. So don't allow sorrow or regret to drag you down. Refuse to give in or give up. Instead, acknowledge God's promise: "My grace is sufficient for you, for My strength is made perfect in weakness" (2 Corinthians 12:9).

Reach out and take hold of God's grace and let Him pull you up from your anxiety and despair. Don't look down at your problems—look up at your all-powerful God. Focus on Him "who is able to do exceedingly abundantly above all that [you] ask or think" (Ephesians 3:20).

A Benediction from the Heart of Paul
Ephesians 3:20-21

Now to Him who is able to do exceedingly
abundantly above all that we ask or think,
according to the power that works in us, to
Him be glory in the church by Christ Jesus to
all generations, forever and ever. Amen.

Chapter 2

Praying for Your Marriage

Husbands, likewise, dwell with them with
understanding, giving honor to the wife, as to the
weaker vessel, and as being heirs together of the
grace of life, that your prayers may not be hindered.

1 PETER 3:7

ut what happened?!"

Have you and your husband ever had this wake-up call in your relationship? Have you experienced a sobering moment when you realized you aren't exactly the same couple you were during the early days and years of your marriage? And you wonder...

"What happened?" One day you and your husband-to-be were best friends. You couldn't wait to get married and be together. And when you were separated, you called each other nonstop. You texted and skyped every minute you had free. Whatever means and methods you could devise, you used all of them to communicate with each other.

Everything focused on your upcoming wedding day. (Afterward, no husband or wife ever forgets that day. Well, your husband may forget the date, but certainly not the event!) If your wedding was like mine, it was a somewhat traditional wedding preceded by months and months of finely tuned planning in preparation for that oh-so-brief ceremony where you repeated vows to each other, pledging to love and honor each other till death do you part.

All of the vows and promises that you made to each other were meant to be binding and were made in the presence of God and multiple witnesses. And the exciting thing is that you and I'm sure your husband meant every word you both uttered. Those vows were not idle statements. They were spoken sincerely from hearts filled with love and devotion. You both genuinely meant every promise you made to each other.

And yet sooner or later the day comes when you look up and wonder, "What happened?"

Well, my friend, what happened, was life. Things don't always turn out the way we think they will when we "fall in love." Life comes along—life with all its ups and downs, trials and triumphs, joys and sorrows, disappointments and failures. Most marriages, including yours as well as mine, experience bumps along the way.

In addition, as time goes along, we tend to forget our wedding vows and what they require of us. It's easy to think of your vows with regard to the other person's obligations and not your own. As a result, if you are not careful, you can eventually begin to view your marriage in terms of yourself and your wants and needs and not about your mate.

So what is the solution? As you continue to pray your way

through your husband's life and his roles and responsibilities, you know by now that you cannot change your husband's attitude about your marriage. But you can change *your* attitude. There are some things you as a wife can do to refocus your heart and thinking on your marriage. The number one thing you can do immediately—right now—is pray for your husband. You can aggressively and faithfully ask God to work in your husband's heart and deal with his actions and his attitude toward your marriage. And, of course, you are actively praying for God to do the same in your heart too!

A Prayer for Your Marriage

In the books Jim and I write on the subject of marriage, I write to wives and point out what God's Word says to wives. In his books, Jim takes on the role of writing to husbands and addresses what the Bible says to husbands.

However, because this book is about the prayers you as a wife pray for your husband, I am using a few scriptures that are directed to husbands. As you go through the prayer that follows, keep in mind it is meant to help you pray for something you *know* is God's will for your husband. Your role is not to use this scripture to chastise your husband or to show him everything in the verse he is failing to do. No, your role is to love your husband and pray and plead with God on his behalf. Then trust God to do the work. When God works in your husband's heart, there will *most definitely* be real change and transformation!

Now for our prayer. Take a minute to read the verse at the top of the opening page of this chapter. Then read on.

My Prayer for My Husband
1 Peter 3:7

Dear Lord, help _____ to realize that we are heirs together of the grace of life, equal spiritual partners. I pray that as _____ and I live togerther, _____ will want to follow Your plan and care for me and honor me as his wife. And Lord, please help me to remember to praise _____ often, and to live out my role as his wife, his partner in life.

As you begin your prayer for your husband and your marriage, you are essentially asking God to remind your husband of five areas of responsibility he is to assume in his marriage relationship with you.

You are praying for your husband's physical relationship with you—"Husbands, likewise, dwell with them." You are praying for your husband to "honor" and be "understanding" of you, but this cannot be separated out from the physical area of your marriage. A true marriage relationship is much more than just sharing the same address. Marriage is fundamentally a physical relationship: "The two shall become one flesh" (Ephesians 5:31). This prayer is as much about intimacy as it is about understanding.

Of course, Christian mates enjoy a deeper spiritual relationship, but the two—physical and spiritual—go together (1 Corinthians 7:1-5). You are asking God to give you a truly spiritual husband who will fulfill his marital roles and love you as Christ loved the church (Ephesians 5:25).

In your prayer that your husband would "dwell" together with you, you are asking God to give your husband a desire to make time to be at home with you and the children. This is a prayer many wives should be praying. In fact, I read somewhere a survey that revealed the average husband and wife spend 37 minutes a week together in actual communication! (I'm not sure I believe this, but you might want to do a little time-log yourself. You might be surprised at how close this survey's conclusion is to the actual time you share real communication with your husband!) If this survey is true, is it any wonder that marriages fall apart after the children grow up and leave home? The husband and wife are left alone—to live under the same roof as strangers!

To "dwell" with a wife also suggests that the husband provides for the physical and material needs of the home. The burden of providing rests on the husband's shoulders (1 Timothy 5:8). But, while it isn't wrong for you as a wife to have a job or career, your first responsibility is to love and care for your husband, children, and your home (Titus 2:4-5).

You are praying for your husband's intellectual relationship with you—God asks husbands to "dwell with them [their wives] with understanding." There are probably at least a thousand and one jokes floating around about a husband's failure to understand his wife, about a husband's lament that he will *never* understand his wife, and about a wife trying in vain to get her husband to understand her. And yet God asks a husband to live with his wife in an understanding way—realizing that...

— she is to be honored as and because she is his wife,

— she is the physically weaker vessel of the two, and

— she is a joint heir with him of the grace of life.

You and your husband also need to understand that you are

not the same people or couple you were when you were first married. Change has occurred. Both of you have gone through a variety of stages and changes during your years together. Your likes and dislikes have changed. New interests and abilities have surfaced. Perhaps children have been added to the mix. You've each been forced to adapt in ways you never imagined.

Here's a simple example. When Jim and I got married, I hated spicy foods. Pepper and onions were foreign substances in my kitchen. Yet today, after living in Southern California with its spicy Mexican flavors in the local food, and living as missionaries in Singapore where chili paste is added to every food item, I now pour on the pepper and slather hot chili paste on just about everything I eat. (But I still feel ill at the smell or taste of dill pickles, which Jim purchases in the largest jars available in the market!)

And I'm sure you and your husband have also developed different tastes, habits, and interests over the years. You've been forced to learn new ways to live due to physical trials, health issues, the makeup of your family unit, the demands of the workplace, financial setbacks...and the list goes on.

The key in your relationship as a couple is making and taking the time to keep up with each other's changes. It's hard to imagine that two married people can live together and not really know each other, but it happens all the time. Ignorance of change and distance are dangerous in any relationship, but they are especially dangerous in a marriage.

And so you must pray! Pray that your husband will be sensitive to your burdens, challenges, feelings, fears, hopes, and dreams—and pray for yourself to do the same. Pray that God will help your husband listen with his heart and share meaningful communication with you. Pray that your home will have an atmosphere of openness and love and submission so that even during the times when the two of you disagree about something, you will still be happy together.

I just have to turn this coin over for a minute and look at the other side, the wife's side and her role and responsibilities. I had to learn—and decide—not to be a whiner. It's easy to whine and complain, to confront or verbally attack your husband for being insensitive and clueless about your "needs." When you and I feel or act in these ways, we need to fall on our knees and pray—for ourselves! God's grace is either sufficient for our trials and challenges and disappointments, or it isn't. And God clearly says it is: "My grace is sufficient for you" (2 Corinthians 12:9). So pray—for yourself first, then for your husband.

Then, after you have prayed, take steps to improve your communication with your husband. Start by heaping praise on your man and being his number one encourager. Be that kind of wife—the one who contributes positively. Then, as one of my mentors taught me, if you have to share something serious, the negative is always on the heels of the positive.

Best of all, be like God's excellent wife in Proverbs 31:26, who "opens her mouth with wisdom, and on her tongue is the law of kindness." These are two of God's good communication principles for wives.

You are praying for your husband's emotional relationship with you—The scripture you are praying goes on to say "giving honor to the wife." When you and your husband-to-be were dating, how did he act? Hopefully, he was attentive and thoughtful, and you were sweet and charming. And after you got engaged, he was probably even more courteous, always the gentleman. All you could see ahead were blue skies, clear sailing, and wedded bliss. And with things going this well, surely things were about to get even better!

But it's sad to say that in time, many brides join the growing number of wives whose husbands have forgotten or neglected to be kind and courteous. Unfortunately, it's easy for a husband to start taking his wife for granted. He fixates on his demanding job and his responsibility to provide for you and any children you have. He forgets that happiness in a home is made up of many little things, including the small courtesies of life.

And so you pray! As you do, pray that your husband remembers to give you honor by respecting your feelings, thoughts, and desires. And remember you are not praying that he will always agree with your ideas or be your special built-in Yes Man. You are praying that he will leave his cares and woes behind and pay more attention to you and your marriage, that he will respect you and your views or opinions.

You are also praying that your husband will acknowledge that the two of you are meant to be a team, that you will both see the wisdom of Ecclesiastes 4:9-12 lived out in your marriage:

> Two are better than one, because they have a good reward for their labor. For if they fall, one will lift up his companion. But woe to him who is alone when he falls, for he has no one to help him up. Again, if two lie down together, they will keep warm; but how can one be warm alone? Though one may be overpowered by another, two can withstand him.

And don't forget to pray to fulfill your roles as a wife. Pray to take seriously your role as your husband's "helper" and that he will see you as his helper (Genesis 2:18).

You are praying for your husband's spiritual relationship with you—"as being heirs together of the grace of life" and "that [his] prayers may not be hindered." If you and your husband are Christians, you are "heirs together." Together you are "joint heirs with Christ" (Romans 8:17). This means that in your roles as Christians you are equal: You submit to one another as joint heirs. Just don't forget that in your marriage, you are to show submission and your husband is to show his love and consideration of you as you both submit to Christ and together follow Him.

You are praying for your husband's priestly relationship with you—"...that [his] prayers may not be hindered." Biblically and historically, the husband was considered to be the "priest" of the family. His job was to pray for and with his wife and children. Job, in the Old Testament, is a powerful biblical example of this priestly role. Job 1:5 tells us that, as the priest of his family, Job "regularly" offered burnt offerings to God according to the number of his children, just in case any of them had sinned.

Wow, this is a lofty prayer request! If your husband is not a Christian, you are to continue to pray for his salvation. And if your husband is nominal in his faith, so much so that you are not sure he is a Christian, pray! And if you have a husband who is sold out to God and on fire for Christ, thank and praise God while you are praying for Him to continue working in your husband's life. Pray that nothing would hinder your husband in his role as priest for your family.

"That your prayers be not hindered" can also speak of your prayers as a couple. Peter assumes that you and your husband pray together. Praying together has a powerful impact on a marriage and can help you bypass many of the usual problems that harm a marital relationship. Here's a thought: If unbelievers can have happy homes and marriages *without prayer* (and many do), how much happier could your Christian marriage and home life be *with prayer?*

And so you pray! According to 1 Peter 3:7, if something is wrong in the marriage relationship, the couples' prayers will be hindered. For that to happen would be serious because you and your family are in a spiritual war against Satan and the world. It is vital that your prayers are not hindered by any sin in your lives. If something is wrong, deal with it quickly—and drastically!

Beyond Prayer, What Can You Do?

I've heard from Jim, my dad, and my three brothers that when a sports team starts losing games, the coach will take the team back to the basic mechanics of how they started the season. The reason for their losing is that somewhere along the way, the team lost sight of the fundamentals of their sport.

I tried to learn how to play golf several times when I was in my twenties, but I was never good at it. But I have often talked to real—and good—golfers who have said that whenever they start playing badly, they go back to the fundamentals of the game. Somewhere along the way, their swing or their putting had altered from how they were trained.

Marriage is likely no different. Getting back to those early days in your relationship with your husband may be all that's needed to solve any problems you might be having. You started out as friends, became best friends, then finally committed to being best friends forever! So beyond praying, what can you do to rekindle your best-friends-forever status with your husband?

As we answer this question, obviously some of the suggestions that follow won't be possible if your husband is not a Christian, or if he is only nominal in his beliefs.

But whether your husband is a Christian or not, you are going to keep praying for him. That's your assignment from God. You can also pray to pay closer attention to your own actions and attitudes. And you can pray to make sure you are following God's four guidelines for all wives—help him, follow him, show respect for him, and love him.[1]

Pray together. Suggest to your husband that the two of you start small with brief prayers together. Jim and I keep a short list of people who need prayer today, right now. We also have an ongoing list of loved ones and people who populate our days. Maybe you can start in this simple way and see what happens. But whatever you do, don't push...or nag...or have expectations. And if it happens, throw your arms around your husband's neck and say, "Thank you!"

Work on common interests. When you were dating, there was so much you enjoyed doing together. But with marriage, unless you both work at it, you can easily drift apart. He has his job, friends, interests, and hobbies. You have the children, neighborhood friends, girlfriends, family, and maybe a job as well. First thing you know, you and your sweetie seem to have nothing in common, especially after the children have left home. Well, it's time to make the effort to start thinking of interests you have in common—things you can do together.

Develop couple goals. Goals are a great way to bring you and your hubby closer together. They give you both a common purpose. Setting goals causes you to think about yourselves as a couple and about the future you would like to work toward—together. You can talk and plan for everything from your next vacation to anniversary or changes you would like to make in your lifestyle. Goals are something positive you can work on together, and celebrate when they are achieved.

Spend time alone together. When our marriage hit the ten-year mark, Jim and I attended a marriage conference. One of the suggestions was that each couple go out on a date every week. Well, you can imagine all the excuses both the men and women began to express. They didn't have the money, didn't have the time, didn't have a babysitter...the list was endless.

Jim and I were right in there with the same excuses—and more! I thought, *Well, if we need to talk, we can do it right in the privacy of our own home, right?* But home is not a good place to have serious, intimate talks about important issues. Long story short? We looked at our calendars and spotted the best time each week, made the effort to find a babysitter, and found a local fast food place that offered endless cups of coffee or soda. We were amazed at how productive and satisfying a date night could be!

Endure suffering together. This one is not something you would wish on anyone, especially yourself. But trials and suffering are a part of everyone's life. Mutually shared heartache has a way of bearing fruit that cannot be produced in any other soil. Whenever the two of you go through a time of physical or emotional suffering, you draw closer together through the experience. One benefit of trials is experiencing together the strength and comfort that comes from the Lord Himself. That was Paul's message in 2 Corinthians 1:3-5:

Blessed be the God and Father of our Lord Jesus Christ, the Father of mercies and God of all comfort, who comforts us in all our tribulation, that we may be able to comfort those who are in any trouble, with the comfort with which we ourselves are comforted by God. For as the sufferings of Christ abound in us, so our consolation also abounds through Christ.

Grow together. It's no fun growing (intellectually and spiritually) and not having your spouse grow along with you. Sooner or later, one of you will be left behind, and you won't have many things you can talk about and enjoy as a couple. This doesn't mean you must be studying or reading or participating in the same areas or interests—or following the same sport or football team. But it does mean you always have something to share with him, and he has something to share with you. There's a spark whenever you get together at the end of the day and have something to talk about—what did you read today? What did you learn? What did you accomplish? This is especially important in the spiritual area of life as you each grow separately and compound that growth by sharing mutual spiritual interests and considering one another "in order to stir up love and good works" (Hebrews 10:24).

Have fun together. I have to tell on myself here! For *years* I planned every Sunday for the week to come. I had our lives down to seven categories that I meticulously planned for each week: spiritual, physical, financial, mental, personal, family, and home. I faithfully listed things to do and projects to work on under each category. That way the urgent things got done and progress was made on things that were more in the future. One

Sunday afternoon while I was working on my master plan for the next week, Jim leaned over with a pen in hand and said, "I'd like to add a category to this list." Then he penned in the word *fun.*

Do you remember how much fun you had while you were dating your spouse and in the early years of your marriage? Then sometime later you began to wonder, *When did life get so serious?* Well, that's what happened to Jim and me. And the epilogue to our story is, together we started planning in some fun!

Speak in the plural. Have you ever had a conversation with a woman who, by the way she is talking, you can't tell whether she is married or single? Sure, she has a ring on her finger, but as she talks, everything she says is "my daughter," "my house," "my last vacation." I always wonder, *Hey, aren't you part of a married couple?*

A mentor of mine taught me the lesson of speaking in the plural. She married for the first time at age 47, and immediately went from being an independent woman and CEO to being a wife. And amazingly, her language changed overnight as everything in her life became "we." For instance, when someone asked her "Where do you live?" her answer was "We live in San Diego." The more time I spent with her, the more I got the "we" message!

You and your husband are a couple. Your life now has a partner. You now have joint interests. So it's "our house," "our daughter," "our vacation." Say along with Joshua: "As for me and my house, we will serve the Lord" (Joshua 24:15). Then back up your talk with your actions by always worshiping together, praying together, and serving together, walking through life arm in arm, facing and enjoying life's challenges—as one. That's exactly where you want to be, and what you want to be.

A Word About Marriage
from the Heart of God

Genesis 2:24

*A man shall leave his father and mother
and be joined to his wife,
and they shall become one flesh.*

Chapter 3

Praying for Your Husband as a Father

Shepherd the flock of God which is among you, serving as overseers, not by compulsion but willingly...nor as being lords over those entrusted to you, but being examples to the flock.

1 PETER 5:2-3

𝓘'm sure you already know this, but let me shout it out from my heart: "God is amazing!" It doesn't matter where you turn—you can't miss the amazing handiwork of the Creator. And there's no doubt that the most amazing part of His creative handiwork was the creation of man and woman. What is overwhelming about this feat is that God created us in His own image. He said, "Let Us make man in Our image, according to Our likeness" (Genesis 1:26).

Just as you and I were "created" physically by an earthly father, in a spiritual sense God is our Father through creation too. In fact, many times the Bible refers to God as "Father." Jesus also referred to God as "our Father in heaven" (Matthew 6:9). This makes the concept of fatherhood extremely important as it applies to the human family, and that includes your family.

As we come to another verse to pray for our husbands—this time as the father of our children—we have much to learn from a scripture that accurately depicts how God models His role as our heavenly Father. We can begin to get a glimpse of what God expects of His earthly fathers, which includes your husband if or when you have children.

My very first thought when I think of God's fatherly care for His children is Psalm 23:1, which states, "The LORD is my shepherd; I shall not want." In this one psalm—in only six verses— our heavenly Father delivers twelve promises to us, His children. In a mere 117 words (depending on your Bible translation), God promises to care for and provide for us, to give us rest and peace, to heal us and guide us. He assures us of His 24/7/forever presence! And He tells us that we will find comfort and friendship, protection and hope in Him. And you know what? This is all we need, and He provides all of it!

That is what God, the Father, does for us—and what He models for earthly fathers to do for their children.

Every Flock Needs a Shepherd

Let's begin by looking at a verse that describes the act and manner of shepherding a flock. Then we'll see how it can then be applied as you pray for your husband in his God-given role as a shepherd and a father.

> Shepherd the flock of God which is among you, serving as overseers, not by compulsion but

willingly...nor as being lords over those entrusted to
you, but being examples to the flock (1 Peter 5:2-3).

These insightful verses were written by the apostle Peter, who
for sure knew a lot about the subject matter at hand. After all,
he was one of the 12 disciples. He had personally watched and
witnessed Jesus shepherding His followers for three years. And
after Jesus rose from the dead, He appeared to the disciples
and spoke directly to Peter. What was the Lord's message to
him? Three times, Jesus told him the same thing:

"Feed My lambs" (John 21:15).

"Tend My sheep" (verse 16).

"Feed My sheep" (verse 17).

Before Jesus left earth and ascended into heaven, He repeated
His message to Peter three times to made sure he understood his
responsibilities as a shepherd: Take care of my flock!

And here in our passage addressing the role of father (1 Peter
5:2-3), as Peter closed the book of 1 Peter, he did exactly what
his Lord had done. Peter delivered a final exhortation and passed
on what Jesus told him: He addressed church leaders regarding
their responsibilities as shepherds to those in the church. Note
this checklist for pastors, leaders—and dads!

The ministry of a shepherd—"Feed the flock." This is what
the word *shepherd* entails. The duties of church leaders include
feeding, leading, encouraging, mentoring, and guarding their
flocks. A shepherd's ministry is to take on the oversight of his
people and be their leader.

You, like the apostle Peter, are to desire that your husband will see himself in this same pastoral and shepherding role with his flock—with his children. And so you pray!

And here's something else to pray for. In order to "feed the flock," your husband must first have something to "feed" his children. So make it a priority to pray that your husband—your children's father—will realize that he must first have God's Word in his heart so he can pass it on to his children's hearts. That is the clear message of God's command to parents in Deuteronomy 6:6-7:

> These words which I command you today shall be in your heart. You shall teach them diligently to your children, and shall talk of them when you sit in your house, when you walk by the way, when you lie down, and when you rise up.

With God's words in *his* heart, your husband can then "teach them diligently" to your children.

The motive of a shepherd—"...not by compulsion but willingly." As was true of Peter, the shepherd must serve the Lord with a willing heart. He should fulfill his role because he loves Christ and the flock, not because he has a job to do. For you, being a mother is a high calling. You know in your heart that your children are not a *job* you are required to fulfill. They are your flesh and blood, the children of your heart. And the same motive should be true of your husband.

And so you pray! Pray that your husband will see being a father to his children as his high calling and own it. Pray that he will realize that being a father is his greatest mission, joy, purpose, and reward. Pray that he doesn't see being a dad as just another duty or obligation, but as a privilege given to him by God.

The manner of a shepherd—"...nor as being lords." Just as church leaders are not to act as dictators, you should pray that your husband will be sensitive and discern the right balance between love and discipline. Paul spoke of this balance when he issued this warning and exhortation to dads: "Fathers, do not provoke your children to wrath, but bring them up in the training and admonition of the Lord" (Ephesians 6:4).

In his book *A Dad After God's Own Heart*, my husband Jim says this about the balance a dad needs to have:

> Your children need your dual role of love and discipline.
>
> Love without discipline is sentimentality.
>
> Discipline without love is bondage.
>
> God's dad keeps these two actions of love and discipline in their proper balance.[1]

Herein lies another prayer request for you to lay before God on behalf of your husband—so pray away!

The stewardship of a shepherd—"...over those entrusted to you." Hebrews 13:17 tells us that church leaders "must give account." They are not to take their positions lightly. Why? Because God is holding them responsible for how they lead their flock. If you are like most church members, you pray regularly for your pastoral staff. And the same should be true of praying for your husband's understanding and execution of his stewardship of his children.

Church leaders must give account to the people, to their board, to their denomination—and most of all, to God! And your husband too will one day give an accounting to God for the children God entrusted to him, for his diligent care and oversight of them as their father.

And so you pray!

The responsibility of a shepherd—"...being examples to the flock." Church leaders are to be responsible examples. After all, we know that the best way to get people to follow you is to set the pace yourself. A pastor is not to demand respect; rather, he is to command it by the godly life he lives and by his sacrificial service. And the same is true for dads too.

And so you pray! In 1 Timothy 4:12, the apostle Paul told Timothy, his disciple and son in the faith, six ways he should live as a positive example to those in his church. Paul wrote, "Be an example to the believers

> in word,
> in conduct,
> in love,
> in spirit,
> in faith,
> in purity."

And so you pray! God's Word has provided in 1 Timothy 4:12 a prayer list you can use as you pray for your husband's character and conduct in *all* his roles and relationships—especially in the most important ones of all, those with his children.

Your Husband as a Shepherd

Are you wondering why I chose a verse that speaks of shepherds and shepherding a flock as a verse for you to pray for your husband? I know for a fact that many people have never seen a sheep, except maybe at a zoo or petting zoo. And it's pretty rare to see an actual shepherd herding and tending to sheep.

I had the surprise of my life when I interviewed for a job in a town on the outskirts of Los Angeles County. After stopping at the gate to gain entrance to the acreage of the Brandeis Institute, I drove down a long road leading away from all signs of city life. And there, for the first time, I found myself personally witnessing a shepherd—complete with a for-real sheepdog—moving flocks of sheep! Well, for more than a year I worked at this kibbutz-style Jewish institute in Simi Valley. Often I was stopped on my way in or out because the shepherd was herding the flocks of sheep across the road to a site with water and green pastures.

Yes, sheep and shepherds still exist in our modern-day world! And yet the idea of shepherding is generally a foreign concept for most people, especially those who live in cities. You don't come across many shepherds and sheep hanging out in Times Square in New York City or Pershing Square in downtown Los Angeles. And for sure you won't see many shepherds leading their flocks down the Magnificent Mile of Chicago. So why and how does the emphasis and analogy of a shepherd help us understand and pray for our husband's role as a father?

First, shepherding is a part of biblical culture. A shepherd fulfilled a vital function for the agrarian people in biblical times because of the prevalence of so many sheep. Even today those who inhabit the Middle East continue to do what they have done for thousands of years. Seeing shepherds and sheep is an everyday sight, a way of life.

But even more important and thrilling is the fact Jesus provided the perfect role model of what a shepherd does, and by extension, what a father is to do in his care for his children. In John 10:11, Jesus referred to Himself as "the good shepherd," and throughout John 10, Jesus spoke of what He did as a shepherd. These activities and His personal example provide many parallels that can help fathers today, as well as help you as you pray for your husband as a dad.

My Prayer for My Husband
1 Peter 5:2-3

Heavenly Father, I come before You now to pray for _____, the father of my children. I pray for _____ to see himself as the shepherd of the flock You have placed in his life—our children. Give _____ Your love and wisdom as he leads as a loving shepherd of our flock, not as a lord over them, and not because he has to, but willingly and joyfully. May _____ set a godly example in our family.

Your Husband's Role as a Shepherd

I hope you are appreciating the beautiful picture Scripture sketches in both John 10 and 1 Peter 5 of what it means to be a good shepherd and what a good shepherd does for his flock.

A shepherd leads his flock—While speaking of the role of a shepherd, Jesus said, "He calls his own sheep by name and leads them out. And when he brings out his own sheep, he goes before them; and the sheep follow him" (John 10:3-4). There is no doubt this description clearly presents a shepherd as being a leader of his flock. And, just as sheep need a leader, your children need their father to lead them. Most men are involved on some level of leadership at their jobs. A good place to begin your prayers is by praying that your husband will see that leading his family is even more important than being a leader at work.

A shepherd is willing to endure hardship for his sheep—In the Old Testament, Jacob told his uncle what he had physically endured to care for Laban's sheep. "There I was! In the day the drought consumed me, and the frost by night, and my sleep departed from my eyes" (Genesis 31:40). God's dad willingly endures hardship for his children. In another chapter in this book I mention that at one time in our marriage, Jim held down four jobs in order to provide for me and our daughters. He never complained, and throughout that difficult time he happily endured hardship. And I knew he would have been willing to do even more if that was what it took for our family—his little flock—to be safe and cared for.

A shepherd is responsible for protecting his flock—The boy David is perhaps the most famous shepherd in the Old Testament. Later, David became the second king of Israel. Many of his psalms were written while watching over his family's flocks. Like most shepherds, David was extremely protective of the sheep in his charge. He even related how he had "killed both lion and bear" to faithfully carry out his duty of protecting of his father's sheep (1 Samuel 17:34-36).

A father not only provides protection for his family against the dangers of physical harm. He also applies vigilant watch and protection in the spiritual realm. He fiercely guards over his children's hearts.

And so you pray! Pray that your husband will see himself as your children's spiritual shepherd and protector as well as their physical shepherd and provider.

A shepherd provides for his flock—The most famous psalm in the Old Testament is Psalm 23. This well-known, popular, and often-quoted passage is frequently referred to as the Shepherd's Psalm. It begins with these familiar and comforting words: "The Lord is my shepherd; I shall not want" (verse 1).

Throughout this psalm God is seen as a loving shepherd who always provides for His flock. David, the writer, viewed God's provision in a very personal way as he referred to God as "my shepherd." Thankfully, most men see their number one priority as providing for their family. This is as it should be, according to 1 Timothy 5:8, which states quite strongly: "If anyone does not provide for his own, and especially for those of his household, he has denied the faith and is worse than an unbeliever."

The shepherd knows his flock—David's personal shepherding imagery continued on into the New Testament to the greatest shepherd of all, the Lord Jesus Christ. Jesus declared, "I am the good shepherd; and I know My sheep, and am known by My own" (John 10:14). Absence does not make the heart grow fonder.

And so you pray for your husband to be involved in the lives of his children. You pray he will grow so close to them that he knows all about them—their hopes, their dreams, their fears, and most of all, their relationships with God. Your husband's physical presence and personal awareness will be the greatest ways he can influence them. And, as an added bonus, as he is with his flock, he is modeling God's character as their caring heavenly Father.

The shepherd is willing to sacrifice himself for his flock. Using your imagination, try to visualize David when he was about 12 years old and had a sword in hand, doing battle with wild beasts as he placed his body between his sheep and the vicious animals, fully ready and willing to sacrifice himself to protect his flock.

Now recall the ultimate sacrifice of the good shepherd, Jesus, as He stated His resolve: "I am the good shepherd. The good shepherd gives His life for the sheep" (John 10:11). Jesus, the ultimate shepherd, willingly laid down His life for His sheep. You and I both know that our husbands would, without hesitation, be willing to give their lives for their children. So as you pray for your incredible husband, don't forget to thank God for the kind of commitment he has to you and your children. You've got a real hero right there under your own roof! Then whisper a prayer that God will help your husband not only be willing to *die* for his family, but be willing to sacrifice himself to *live* for and with his children. Pray for him to be willing to sacrifice...

— his time for time with his children

— his interests for the interests of his children

— his fun for having fun with his children

— his comfort for the comfort of his children

— his finances for the future of his children[2]

Jacob and David and Peter, and most especially God and Jesus, show us what a good shepherd looks like. In them we see models of how God desires a dad to interact with his family. The concept of a shepherd is thousands of years old, yet even today it still illustrates—beautifully and powerfully—your husband's role as a father.

Beyond Prayer, What Can You Do?

Prayer is precious. It is also work. But one thing I relish about time spent in prayer is it usually occurs when all is quiet!

This can happen early in the morning when your world is still and dark. Or it can happen later, after your husband and children have vacated the house and you are left home alone with a blessed quietness. I'm not saying we don't sometimes cry our hearts out and unburden all of our sorrows and worries and stresses when we pray. After all, what else can we do with them?! But generally, prayer takes place in the natural, normal flow of a day. It's you and God, you worshiping and God listening as you commune and talk over your life and your day—and your husband—with the Lord.

But sooner or later, prayer time is over and you need to rise up and face the day and its realities. You've prayed for your husband: Check. Now what can you do beyond praying for him?

1. *Encourage your husband in his role as father*—Take every opportunity to let your husband know how much you appreciate his involvement with the children. Ask him if he's okay with you setting up some family activities and outings. And ask him if he has suggestions and ideas for these get-togethers. One of our favorites was a family slumber party in sleeping bags right in our own living room—complete with flashlights and, of course, lots of snacks! You can also suggest that the two of you read a parenting book together or take a parenting class at church so you both can be better parents.

2. *Talk with your husband about ways each of you can be with the children*—Help him find the time to be with the children. You could suggest that he take each of the children on an outing by themselves once in a while. If he has a time-consuming job (and what husband doesn't!), suggest that he take one or all the kids with him when he runs errands. These local jaunts might just be one of the few times he can truly spend with one or all

of the children all week! Maybe (and I know this requires more time and a lot of patience) you can suggest that as he works on or washes the car, or works on the lawn and yard or house, he could include one of the kids. As they work together he will have opportunity not only to teach them, but to enjoy one-on-one conversations.

3. *Assist your husband in his role as spiritual leader*—How? Schedule the preparations for bedtime so dad has time to be with the children. They can have a tickle match, read from a book, and maybe he can even see that the family prays together, or if it works out, he can pray with each child during the end of the day tucking-in time.

And the same goes for the morning routine. If possible, adjust the schedule so the family can have devotions together. Your commitment to preparing and working ahead of schedule, getting the family up and to the table, having breakfast set out along with a Bible and whatever material you are using for devotions, can make this dream of a family devotional time come true! You know your family's unique schedule. For many, dad leaves for work at 0-dark-thirty and cannot join the family for breakfast. So pray and figure out what would work for you and yours. And when your husband can't be there, you and the kids can pray for dad's day, and you can fill his shoes at devotional time until he's back.

4. *Support your husband in his role as father*—Just as I am to honor and submit to my heavenly Father, I am also commanded to honor and submit to my husband. Take every opportunity to let your children see you helping, following, respecting, and loving your husband. Demonstrate to your children how they

are to do the same with their father. In fact, expect and require them to "honor" their father (Exodus 20:12 and Ephesians 6:2).

Praying for our husbands always comes back to ourselves, doesn't it? We cannot pray for our husbands to possess any character quality or exhibit any kind of godly behavior that we are not displaying ourselves. And so we pray! Pray for yourself, my dear sister in Christ. Then pour out those prayers for your husband and his role as a father.

An Extra Prayer to Pray from the Heart of Paul

Ephesians 6:4

Help _____ to train and teach his children
in the nurture and admonition of the Lord.
Enable him to do this without
provoking them to anger.

Chapter 4

Praying for Your Husband's Wisdom

The heart of the wise teaches his mouth,
and adds learning to his lips.

PROVERBS 16:23

𝓘f you could pray for one thing beyond your husband's salvation, what would you want for him above all else?

This is the same question asked of King Solomon in the Old Testament, and it was asked by God! God spoke to Solomon, saying, "Ask! What shall I give you?"

Solomon's answer? "Give me wisdom."

"Give Me Wisdom"

Solomon was the son of the wealthy and mighty King David of Israel. When Solomon became Israel's king, he was somewhat young (1 Kings 3:7) and up till then, had lived in his father's larger-than-life shadow. He was definitely inexperienced.

Hopefully you will take some time to read Solomon's full story in 1 Kings 1:1–11:43.

At this time in Solomon's life, it's entirely possible he may have been quaking in his sandals and staggering under the weight of his new responsibilities. For whatever reason, God came to Solomon in the night and prompted, "Ask! What shall I give you?" (2 Chronicles 1:7). Like the rest of all humanity, Solomon could have been tempted to ask for the moon—for riches, for a conquering army, for a long life, for lots of "things." Instead, Solomon answered,

> Give me wisdom and knowledge, that I may go out and come in before this people; for who can judge this great people of Yours? (verse 10).

Obviously God was pleased with Solomon's request. He said to Solomon:

> Because this was in your heart, and you have not asked riches or wealth or honor or the life of your enemies, nor have you asked long life—but have asked wisdom and knowledge for yourself, that you may judge My people over whom I have made you king—wisdom and knowledge are granted to you (verses 11-12).

Then came the bonus!

> ...and I will give you riches and wealth and honor, such as none of the kings have had who were before you, nor shall any after you have the like (verse 12).

It's no wonder Solomon became the wisest man who ever

lived (other than Jesus Christ, of course). He is heralded as the man who spoke 3000 proverbs (1 Kings 4:32). In the book of Proverbs you can read the best of his 3000 wise sayings. He was truly brilliant: "God gave Solomon wisdom and exceedingly great understanding" (1 Kings 4:29).

What Is Wisdom?

Before we address praying for wisdom for our husbands, let's learn more about wisdom—what it is, why we need it, and why we should desire it and pray for it.

I'm sure you know this scenario: All day long, every single day, decisions come at you almost by the second! Sometimes you feel like life's demands are bombarding you on all fronts. And every assault calls for something from you—a word, an answer, a judgment call, an action, a choice, a decision. You have to decide what to think or not think, say or not say, ask or let lie, work on or wait on. In a word, you need the same thing you are praying for your husband—you need wisdom! So where do you find it?

Wisdom has its source in God—Everything has a source. It starts somewhere...as my family discovered one day while driving through the state of Montana. While on a long stretch of road, we drove over a short little bridge with a sign that read, "Missouri River."

"What!" a chorus went up from all four of us at the same time. We had been to St. Louis and seen the impressive width of the Missouri River just before it empties into the mighty Mississippi. And yet, this river in Montana was small—only a little more than a creek. So Jim backed up the car to make certain we hadn't misread the sign. Sure enough, it was the beginnings of the Missouri River. We weren't far from its source.

Here's something to ponder: Everything has a source...except God. God is the source of all things. Chances are you already know that the heavens and earth have their source in God (Genesis 1:1). But did you know that wisdom has its source in God too? God *is* wisdom (Ezra 7:25). And His wisdom and knowledge are derived from no one (Job 21:22). All true wisdom has its source in God. So, as one who needs wisdom for any and all of your roles and responsibilities, you can look to God and His Word for wisdom.

Wisdom is more than knowledge—You've probably met some really smart people who impressed you when you first met them. But, in time, as you got to know them better, you began to realize there was very little connection between their knowledge and wise living. Their ability to make good decisions wasn't all that great. Why? They lacked wisdom.

By contrast, there are many people who have received little or no formal training, yet they possess great wisdom and make good decisions.

The use of the wisdom presented in God's Word requires no formal education. It is simply the proper application of knowledge. It is the ability to think clearly and make good decisions—even in the midst of difficult situations and emergencies.

Like most people, you probably think you could use more of this kind of wisdom. Well, I have some good news for you—God offers this wisdom to you freely! Read on.

Wisdom is available—Are you experiencing any problems or trials in your life? Are you at a crossroads in your career? Could you use some direction in your relationship with your husband, or a family member or a friend or workmate? Are you struggling through some issues as a wife and mother? Then you need wisdom—God's wisdom, and there's no need to wait even another second for it. God has promised you wisdom. He calls out in James 1:5:

> Your problem—*If any of you lacks wisdom*
>
> God's instructions—*let him ask of God*
>
> Encouragement—*who gives to all liberally and without reproach*
>
> God's promise—*and it will be given to him*

My praying friend, whatever issue or problem you are facing, you don't have to argue, debate, make lists of possible positive and negative outcomes. You don't have to wrestle with your views and thoughts for days or weeks on end. You don't have to agonize or grope around in the dark, hoping to stumble upon answers through trial and error. Whenever you need wisdom, all you need to do is pray and *ask of God*...and He will respond: *It will be given* to you!

Wisdom is freely given—Have you and your husband ever had to ask for a loan? The loan officer probably took a lot of time with your application. He may have exercised such great caution you began to think it was his own money he was lending you! Having to make such a request can be agony, and even embarrassing, as your spending habits and debts are revealed and your credit rating is checked, and all the cold hard facts are laid out. If you're at all like me, you probably walked away hoping you would never have to go through *that* experience again!

God's response to your requests for wisdom is just the opposite. He *gives to all liberally*. He doesn't merely dole out wisdom "here a little, there a little, everywhere a little little." And He doesn't make you wait in line to receive it. And He doesn't give it grudgingly. No, He *gives to all* who ask. Plus He gives His wisdom *liberally*—freely, generously, and with an open hand.

God also doesn't dole out a lecture every time you come to Him asking, "May I have some more wisdom, please?" No, each time you ask, wisdom is given *without reproach*. With this kind of promise, and with this kind of freedom, why, oh why aren't we beating a path to God on a regular basis?

Wisdom comes in a variety of ways—While the Missouri River has one source, it also has many tributaries that add to its size and power as it flows toward its destiny, the mighty Mississippi. What "wisdom tributaries" does God feed into your life to strengthen and mature you, to make you wise? Here are three to get you started.

— *Your walk with God.* Wisdom comes as you develop God-awareness, as you walk with the Lord and follow Him daily, as you grow a more conscious, worshipful attitude toward Him. The foundation of wisdom is to "fear...the Lord" (Proverbs 1:7). As you honor and esteem God, live in awe of His power, and obey His Word, His wisdom becomes your wisdom. It's yours as you walk with Him and He becomes the controlling influence in your life.

A pearl of wisdom for you: Going to church and worshiping God starts your week off with the right focus and a dose of His wisdom.

— *Your time in God's Word.* God's Word can make you wise—wiser than your enemies, your teachers, even some who are older than you. How can you get this wisdom? It's simple—know God's Word and obey it (Psalm 119:98-100).

A pearl of wisdom for you: Going through a devotional with your husband helps you both get into the Bible and grow. Digging into God's Word daily will get the Bible into you.

— *Your input from others.* You can gain wisdom through seeking the advice of those who possess it. That's one powerful reason you are praying for wisdom for your husband. It would be an incredible resource to have a husband who is filled with wisdom and is handy when life gets complicated! You can also read the wise and godly advice of others through Christian books, Bible studies, blogs, and newsletters. Seeking the wisdom of others helps you grow in maturity. So, as Proverbs 4:5 says, "Get wisdom!"

A pearl of wisdom for you: Pray for mentors for both you and your husband. Ask God to show you who might be available to help you. And look online to see what books can help you advance in wisdom. Obviously the truest, purest, most reliable source of wisdom is God's Word, the Bible.

A Woman of Amazing Wisdom

If you have read any of my books, you know how much I love studying the women of the Bible. Well, I want you to meet a woman who shows us the beauty—and the benefits—of wisdom. In contrast to King Solomon, she was not in a leadership position and did not have a prestigious title. No, she was a wife and home manager. But she possessed a great measure of wisdom—wisdom that not only bettered her hard and bitter life, but saved it and the lives of many! Her name was Abigail, and her story is told in 1 Samuel 25:1-42.

Abigail was married to an alcoholic tyrant named Nabal (meaning "fool"). We can only imagine the tightrope Abigail walked every day. Yet she is applauded as a woman of wisdom. Her most amazing act of wisdom was averting a bloodbath between her foolish husband and the avenging warrior David and his 400 men. Abigail knew when to act...and did. She knew what to do...and did it. And she knew what to say...and said it.

What are some of the marks of Abigail's wisdom? She...

> ...perceived the big picture,
>
> ...kept her composure,
>
> ...formed a plan,
>
> ...spoke with wisdom, and
>
> ...effectively influenced others.

Abigail's life teaches us that every challenge or responsibility that lies before us can be handled in a better way and lead to a better outcome when it is handled with God's wisdom.

A Prayer for Wisdom

As we come to this next prayer for our husbands, notice it was written by Solomon, who is passing on the wisdom that was given to him by God. Look now at this verse for a greater understanding of what wisdom will do for your husband—and you.

> The heart of the wise teaches his mouth,
> and adds learning to his lips (Proverbs 16:23).

Wisdom proceeds from the heart—"The heart of the wise

teaches his mouth." The heart is the seat of human emotion. This means that ultimately, every word you speak and every action you perform comes from the heart. When you pray for you and your husband to each grow in wisdom, you are praying for your hearts—that your hearts will be open to the Spirit's leading, that they will be filled with God's wisdom, that they will "teach" wisdom to your mouths.

Think back to the best teachers you had in school. They made the classroom a fun place to be, and you couldn't wait to hear what new information they would share. That's what you are praying for the two of you as a couple. Pray that when your husband opens his mouth, people will be instructed by his wisdom and excited and eager to respond to it.

Wisdom prompts discernment—"The heart of the wise *teaches* his mouth." A wise person is always listening, evaluating, and processing what she sees and hears. She mentally and emotionally appraises it all and is able to get to the heart of an issue—to discern its meaning. Her wisdom results in common sense.

What wife wouldn't desire this skill for herself—and for her husband? Just think, you could go to him with any issue you are facing, and together the two of you could resolve it. With wisdom he would be able to arrive at wise, God-honoring solutions. And as a woman of wisdom, you would be able to offer input as you and your husband work as a team.

Wisdom produces discretion—"...and adds learning to his lips." These words could be translated "causes his mouth to be prudent." A wise person is careful about what he says and how he says it. You are praying for yourself and for your husband's words to be carefully spoken so they help—not hurt. Ephesians 4:29 advises, "Let no corrupt word proceed out of your mouth, but what is good for necessary edification, that it may impart grace to the hearers."

Praying for Wisdom for Your Husband

Take a minute to read Proverbs 16:23, which reveals that wisdom is the answer to any issues you have with your husband and any issues he has with others, both now and in the future.

My Prayer for My Husband
Proverbs 16:23

Father and all-wise One, I pray that _____ will grow in wisdom and become a man marked by great wisdom and common sense, one who teaches his mind, mouth, and body to speak and act carefully and with sensitivity. Move in _____'s heart to "get wisdom." Please, O Lord, give him wisdom to guide our family at home and help the people at his work place.

As you ask God for wisdom for your husband, be specific:

Pray for the "fear of the LORD." Proverbs says, "The fear of the LORD is the beginning of wisdom, and the knowledge of the Holy One is understanding" (9:10). And so you pray! Pray first and foremost for your husband to have a reverential awe of God. This respect for God will move him to submit to God's wisdom in the Bible.

Pray too that your husband will "walk in the Spirit" (Galatians 5:16). The "fear of the LORD" will cause him to be sensitive to the Spirit's leading. This sensitivity and reverence will cause your husband to imitate God's wisdom in his interactions with family, friends, workmates, and the people at your church and in your community.

Pray for a desire for wisdom. You've heard this many times: "You can lead a horse to water, but you can't make it drink." This is why you fervently pray that your husband will want wisdom above all else. The wisdom is there. It's available. But he must *desire* it, just as King Solomon did. He asked for wisdom, for "an understanding heart" (1 Kings 3:9).

Wisdom is a very desirable trait to possess. As Solomon said in another of his wisdom sayings, "Happy is the man who finds wisdom, and the man who gains understanding; for her proceeds are better than the profits of silver, and her gain than fine gold" (Proverbs 3:13-14). Another proverb summarizes, "How much better to get wisdom than gold!" (Proverbs 16:16).

Yes, wisdom calls to all who pass by, but your husband must answer the call. To discover the treasure of wisdom, he must follow God's treasure map, or the Bible: "The LORD gives wisdom; from His mouth come knowledge and understanding" (Proverbs 2:6).

Pray for a receptive heart for wisdom. I'm sure you want to be a woman of wisdom who is wise enough to be a sounding board for your husband. And you want to be a wise marriage partner who has a solid biblical perspective on any issue or challenge he's dealing with. This is why you must pray for wisdom for yourself.

But just as importantly, you need to pray for your husband to be receptive to counsel and advice from mature Christians. Encourage him to choose a "go-to guy" at church, one he can turn to for wisdom whenever he has a question. Wisdom is contagious. A spiritual mentor can guide your husband in the ways of God. He can teach him biblical principles for making wise decisions and speaking with wisdom.

Pray for a lifetime commitment to nurture wisdom. Because life circumstances are always changing, the search for wisdom is a lifelong pursuit. It must be sought day after day. God's gift of wisdom for you and your husband is for today. Use it with His blessings! And tomorrow? Get up and ask for wisdom all over again. Yesterday's wisdom will not be adequate for the issues you face today. And today's wisdom will not be adequate for the issues you face tomorrow. So pursue wisdom continually.

Her Husband Is Known at the Gate

Wisdom seems to come naturally for some people. Maybe your husband is one of these people. Praise God if he is—and pray! As his wife, your job assignment from God is to keep praying for him day in and day out.

Whatever level of wisdom your husband possesses today, your job is to encourage him at every opportunity. When he makes a wise decision, praise him and thank him. When he is undecided about a decision, listen and pray. Ask questions—and pray! Hear him out. If he is about to make a doubtful (in your estimation) decision, once again listen, ask questions, and encourage him to seek the wisdom of others...and pray to God as well.

Your goal is not to hinder your husband, but to be a loving, supportive influence on him. Pray that your husband will become like the Proverbs 31 husband: "Her husband is respected at the city gate, where he takes his seat among the elders of the land" (Proverbs 31:23 NIV).

A Prayer to Pray from the Heart of Solomon

2 Chronicles 1:9-10

Now, O LORD God...give me wisdom and knowledge, that I may go out and come in before this people.

Chapter 5

Praying for Your Husband's Job

*Whatever you do in word or deed, do all in
the name of the Lord Jesus, giving thanks
to God the Father through Him.*

COLOSSIANS 3:17

J love those ads on television in which you see a couple walking along a sandy beach. Their pant legs are rolled up, they are holding hands, and they look happy. We all dream of exotic vacations on a Caribbean cruise or lounging around a shimmering pool at a really, really nice hotel. (And don't forget in that dream to include the full treatment at the spa!)

Well, to carry this daydream a little further, there may have also been a fantasy that marriage would somehow include lots of vacations and plenty of time for leisure. You and your husband would also have plenty of money and lots of time to travel the world and enjoy all sorts of unique experiences.

So, how is your fantasy working out? If you are like most couples, real life is not quite how you pictured it in your mind. Instead of walking on the beach, you and your husband are pounding the streets of your city on your way to work as a salesman, a nurse, a teacher, a warehouse or factory manager, or hurrying to assemble on the parade ground of a military base.

What happened? Kids, rent, braces, schools, college, the list of financial expenses goes on and on and on. Your husband and probably you too are working to just keep your heads above water. Even if you are a stay-at-home mom, you are one busy lady! So no matter what your circumstances, you both have a "job"! He works, but you work too as you manage a bustling household and teeming brood of kids! But, no matter what your particular scenario is, isn't this the way God intended it to be?

Dispelling the Rumor

Rumor has it that work is a consequence of the fall of man—that if Adam and Eve had not eaten that apple, we wouldn't have to work today! But in reality, work existed before the Fall. Long before that first bite of fruit, we witness God at work in the creation of the universe.

In Genesis 1:1, we meet God punching the time clock, so to speak, as a worker: "In the beginning God created the heavens and the earth." Finally, when the work was completed on the seventh day, God "rested from all His work which [He] had created and made" (Genesis 2:3). Then after Adam and Eve were created, God told them to "be fruitful and multiply; fill the earth and subdue it; have dominion over the fish of the sea, over the birds of the air, and over every living thing that moves on the earth" (Genesis 1:28). That sounds like work to me!

So throughout the Bible, beginning with Adam and Eve in the Garden of Eden, work is seen as a normal and natural part of life. The Old Testament book of Proverbs often contrasts work and those who labor with those who don't or won't work and the consequence of their lack of diligence. For instance:

> In all labor there is profit,
> but idle chatter leads only to poverty (Proverbs 14:23).

> Do you see a man who excels in his work?
> he will stand before kings;
> he will not stand before unknown men (22:29)

And let's not forget the woman of Proverbs 31:10-31. Don't tell me this stay-at-home mom didn't work! Here's a sample of this "excellent" wife's activities:

> 13 She seeks wool and flax,
> and willingly works with her hands.
> 14 She is like the merchant ships,
> she brings her food from afar.
> 15 She also rises while it is yet night,
> and provides food for her household,
> and a portion for her maidservants.
> 16 She considers a field and buys it;
> from her profits she plants a vineyard.
> 17 She girds herself with strength,
> and strengthens her arms.
> 18 She perceives that her merchandise is good,
> and her lamp does not go out by night.
> 19 She stretches out her hands to the distaff,
> and her hand holds the spindle...
> 21 She is not afraid of snow for her household,
> for all her household is clothed with scarlet.

²² She makes tapestry for herself;
    her clothing is fine linen and purple...
²⁴ She makes linen garments and sells them,
    and supplies sashes for the merchants...
²⁷ She watches over the ways of her household,
    and does not eat the bread of idleness...
³¹ Give her of the fruit of her hands,
    and let her own works praise her in the gates.

My fellow working friend, it's obvious God created us, both men and women, to be workers. He knows that our physical and mental makeup thrives on work.

The Tale of Two Husbands

As we come to this next verse to pray for your husband, you will be faced with one of two possible directions for your prayers. The two possibilities are Husband #1 and Husband #2. The profiles that follow are deliberately extreme in order to cover the variety of attitudes a man may have toward his work and his job.

Husband #1 loves his job. He is good at it. He is constantly improving in his abilities while at work. His job requires tremendous responsibility, and therefore, he takes his work seriously. You might be thinking, *So what's the problem? I could only wish my husband was more like this guy—this Husband #1!*

Well, as the saying goes, be careful what you wish for. Husband #1 shows many signs that he could become a workaholic. He leaves super early for the job and comes home late. He brings his work home and stays up working on this project or preparing that report. When he is with you and the kids, he is only half there, if that much. Even while you are supposed to be enjoying your family vacation, he's talking multiple times daily with people at the office or with a client. And never mind how many emails and text messages are flying back and forth!

Husband #2, however, does not love his job. In fact, he may even hate it! Maybe he started out liking his work, but somewhere along the way, something happened. His favorite boss retired. Or he reached a dead-end in advancement, or was demoted to a lesser job. Because he is dissatisfied with his job, the family feels the effects of his discontent. Every day is a "bad day at the office," so he comes home, kicks the dog, yells at you, and ignores the children. He becomes withdrawn and spends his time staring at the television. Your happy-go-lucky groom is now angry, depressed, discouraged, and discontent—and he lets you know it.

As I said, I am exaggerating a bit about these two extreme portraits of men on the job. But from my years of ministry to women, I don't think I'm too far off in my portrayals. If you are the wife of either Husband #1 or #2, you know what a challenge you are facing. Obviously, as we have established, you as a wife are called to help your husband (Genesis 2:18)—and to pray for him. You are to pray for your husband and his job, and how it is affecting him. Both Husband #1 and #2 are responding negatively to aspects of their job. How can you help without coming right out and confronting your husband? Before you resort to a scene, start by praying for balance. Our prayer verse is coming right up, so hold on!

Praying for Balance

God wants your husband to be a strong spiritual model and leader for his family as well as a provider. Many husbands fixate on the "providing" part of their husbandly duties and become consumed by their jobs, either as a workaholic or as a man trapped in a job he dislikes but knows he needs in order to care for his family.

Yes, God wants a husband to provide for his family, proclaim his faith, love his family, and pursue his job as a calling from the Lord. But a balance can be reached where your husband doesn't detest his job so much that it affects his relationships at home and his health.

How is all of this possible? And how can balance be attained? There is a natural tension in your husband's life when it comes to his work. He understands that God expects him to provide for his family. He has probably read or heard and understands the implications of the verse that says, "If anyone does not provide for his own, and especially for those of his household, he has denied the faith and is worse than an unbeliever" (1 Timothy 5:8).

I'm sure you can imagine the daily pressure God's mandate places on your husband. Whether you work or not, or whether you contribute in other ways to your family's financial condition, you can ask God daily to act in your husband's heart so he finds balance, peace, joy, fulfilment, and success in his profession. And so you pray!

A Prayer to Pray

Here's an all-encompassing verse to pray for your spouse as an employee and the provider for your family. Be sure to look at the verse in your Bible or on the first page of this chapter. As with each prayer in this book, insert your husband's name in the blanks as you pray. Lift your heart and your words—and your husband!—up to Your Father who is in heaven.

My Prayer for My Husband
Colossians 3:17

Dear Lord, whatever _____ does today in word or deed, I pray that he does it with You in mind and in the name of the Lord Jesus. Guide _____ to live as Your representative, Lord, bringing glory and honor to You by the way he conducts himself. I thank and praise You for _____ and pray that both _____ and I will constantly give thanks to God the Father through Jesus.

This is a perfect prayer to pray for your husband because your request to God is based on a verse straight out of the Bible. Be sure you notice a few special elements within this prayer.

The all-embracing nature of your prayer—"Whatever you do in word or deed, do all..." In these few words, the apostle Paul gives one of the most all-embracing statements in the New Testament. Here we learn what is to govern your husband's Christian life, and yours too. "Whatever" your husband does points to the extent of your prayers and concerns for your man. And here's more good news: The word "whatever" gives you the opportunity to insert whatever you want or whatever is pressing your heart to pray. *Whatever* might be a big meeting your husband is attending or leading. Or it might include a long business trip or deployment. Whatever your "whatever" is, you've got him covered.

Your prayer continues with "in word or deed." This spans your husband's speech and his every activity.

But there's more. For even further emphasis, Paul adds "do all." "Do all" doesn't mean this is a generic "shotgun" prayer like "God, bless my husband today." It's a prayer that allows you to include specifics in your husband's day, like a meeting with the boss. It's more like a "blanket-covering prayer" for whatever may happen in your husband's work day.

The desire of your prayer—Pray that your husband will "do all in the name of the Lord Jesus." Your request is that he will judge and choose his speech and conduct according to God's Bureau of Standards, according to God's standards for appraising his actions—which is "the name of the Lord Jesus."

What does this mean? You are praying that your husband's words and actions will be done in a way that establishes him as a true representative and follower of Jesus Christ. You are praying that his actions will be according to God's will. You are praying that your husband will do everything "to the glory of God" (1 Corinthians 10:31).

The hope of your prayer—"...giving thanks to God the Father through Him." Your prayer concludes with asking God to give your husband a thankful heart in spite of the circumstances of his job. At work there will be pressure and disappointment and great expectations from his employer. There will be long hours and surprise challenges. Or, on the other end of the spectrum, some days his job may lack challenge or he may be asked to do something that makes no sense. Your prayer is that regardless of what he faces, your husband will remember to thank God that he has a job that enables him to provide for his family— that he is doing God's will by working, which always glorifies and pleases God.

And this is a great reminder for you too. Giving thanks to

God the Father through the Lord Jesus is as important for you to remember for yourself as it is for your husband. Life doesn't always go your way. You may be the wife of a man described by Husband #1 or Husband #2. But that never excuses you from your need to be thankful for your blessings.

Beyond Prayer, What Can You Do?

Understand your husband's mandate. God ordained that men are to work and provide for their families. This is seen in the Bible as early as Genesis. Historically, the husband has usually been the breadwinner. But times have changed. When I wrote my first book, *Loving God with All Your Mind,*[1] the majority of women in this country were stay-at-home wives and mothers. Today the majority of married women are now a part of the workforce. Some wives work out of their homes, but many leave home at some time each day for a job.

This change in statistics and lifestyle has certainly taken some pressure off of husbands to be the sole provider. But work is still a part of God's plan for husbands. It's something they must do. Be sure you willfully and regularly support and encourage your husband in his job.

Talk with your husband about his job. It's amazing what you can learn when you have an honest discussion about your husband's job. These times are not meant to be a lemon squeeze or a gripe session. Just ask your husband how he spends the bulk of his time at work. What does he do hour by hour? What kinds of crises occur? What projects is he working on? What does he like most about his job, and what are his challenges?

If your husband is unhappy with his job, you have another issue: What can you do to help him turn his attitude around?

Obviously, getting him to memorize Colossians 3:17 would help influence his attitude in a positive way.

Your husband may even be thinking about changing jobs. If he feels trapped financially, what can you do to help out? One thing you can do is talk about possible solutions on the home front. For instance, you might consider selling a car, or taking the kids out of their private school. Talk about ideas for easing up your financial burdens so your husband can change jobs and still provide for the needs of your family. Do whatever you can to show your support.

Throughout your married life, there will be many changes in your husband's job situation and in your family's financial status. And when you are armed with real information from your talks with him, you will know exactly how to pray each day.

Seek opportunities to talk. I'm sure I'm repeating myself, *but communication is the key to marriage.* Your husband's job is obviously an important part of his life and your marriage. So work out ways the two of you can get away even for an hour or two to talk. Often Jim and I would get a babysitter and walk across the street to a place that served free Coke refills. And you guessed it! We ordered two Cokes and talked to our hearts' content. Another couple we know picked Wednesday evenings as "baked potato night" and went to a fast-food restaurant that had a baked potato bar. In their case and ours, the price was next to nothing. But that was okay because, after all, the time wasn't about the food— it was about communication and growth as a couple. These dates gave us time to talk without distractions on a no-frills budget!

Ask what you can pray for. I always asked Jim, "What's happening at work today?" As he shared, I would take mental notes for prayer. If he had a presentation at 10:00, I set a timer to pray at 10:00. If he had a meeting at 2:00, that went on my prayer schedule for the day. Later that evening I could ask, "How did your meeting go?" I even went through years when I prayed for Jim every hour on the hour, setting my watch to alert me every 60 minutes. As I said in another chapter, as wives we not only pray, but we pray, pray, pray!

Provide lots of praise! With the high stress level of your husband's job and his role as provider, it's music to his ears when you let him know how much you appreciate him and his efforts to take care of you and the family. Pray that the demands of his job don't affect his spiritual life, or his physical health, or the health of the family. Pray that you will be his number one encourager and a rock of support for him. And pray each day that your lips will leak praise to your husband.

Be a neutral sounding board. I personally don't know a single man who has remained in one job for all of his working years. So you can count on it—the day will come when your husband entertains a job change. You need to be his positive sounding board, his closest friend and confidant. Try to be neutral and help him think through the options. He may need to change locations for his profession. He may need to go back to school and change professions.

This is a special time for you to approach God as a prayer warrior on behalf of your husband and family. When your foundation gets shaken, it's easy to fall apart. This is when you remember to turn to God—every time you worry, every time you are anxious, every time you get that panicky feeling that your world is falling apart. If you and I feel like this, imagine how your husband is feeling with such a major burden on his shoulders. And so you pray.

A Personal Story

I know a L-O-T about hard times and life changes. Jim and I married in college and completed our educations without financial support from our parents. It's not that they didn't want to help out—they simply didn't have the money to help us.

When I met Jim on campus, we both had part-time jobs that we kept until graduation. And since then, we have known only a very few years when we didn't both work in some way to take care of our daughters and living expenses. I worked away from home until we had children. Then I worked at home doing transcription, bookkeeping, and other office-type work. Believe me, we saw our lives turned upside down almost every other year as Jim was transferred every 18 months for his job. He was even activated into military service during Operation Desert Storm and the Bosnian crisis.

But I learned the most about supporting my husband's job during ten very lean years. That decade began when Jim resigned from his job as a pharmaceutical salesman to enter seminary to prepare for the ministry. As you can imagine, those were some tough years. And our daughters remember those years too. One day my Katherine, a newlywed at that time, called and asked, "Mom, do you have any of those recipes you used to fix when we were on hard times?"

I think a lot about those challenging years. Well, one morning I was wondering how I made it through those trying times. Actually, it was a trying *decade!* So I looked through my prayer notebook, located those years, and read through my prayer lists. And there I discovered my prayer requests for my Jim, who had four—yes, *four*—part-time jobs so I could stay at home with our two preschoolers. Instead of being bitter and dwelling on the plenty we had enjoyed in the past, we had adjusted. Jim took on extra work, and I did everything I could do to keep spending to a minimum.

And...I prayed. I prayed like crazy. I felt like the man who shared the following experience, which I believe is the way God wants us to live: "In a single day I have prayed as many as a hundred times, and in the night almost as often."[2]

May our Lord richly bless you and yours, my sweet friend, as you reach out to Him with your heart and your needs. May He shower you with His grace and favor as you pray and support and love your husband!

A Word About Prayer from the Heart of Paul

Philippians 4:6-7

*Be anxious for nothing, but in everything by prayer
and supplication, with thanksgiving, let your
requests be made known to God; and the peace
of God, which surpasses all understanding, will
guard your hearts and minds through Christ Jesus.*

Chapter 6

Praying for Your Husband's View of Money

The love of money is a root of all kinds of evil, for which some have strayed from the faith in their greediness, and pierced themselves through with many sorrows.

1 TIMOTHY 6:10

I have always heard that money problems are at the base of the majority of arguments and disagreements in a marriage. And sure enough, when I typed in "What are the top ten problems in marriages?" on my Internet search site, almost every list created by both marriage counselors and divorce lawyers had finances right up there at the top as number one!

Just pick up any newspaper or magazine or read your online world news link and you will immediately know that marriage is not the only institution having money problems. Government committees and leaders, businesses both large and small, and even many churches get trapped into thinking money is the answer to every problem.

And it's no different for your marriage and family. It's so easy—and natural—to mistakenly think, *If we just had more money, we could have a car that isn't more than a decade old. We could live in a nicer neighborhood, and our kids could attend a better school. And just think of the bonding that could occur if we had enough money to go on a real vacation!*

Many working wives also think, *If we had more money, I could quit my job and take care of things at home and be a better wife and mom.*

On and on our daydreams, wishes, rationalizations, and justifications go. This kind of thinking can only lead to the conclusion that in order to feed our desires, however noble or fun we think they might be, we will need more money—and the more the better, and the sooner the better!

"If God Didn't Meet It, I Didn't Need It"

Part of our testimony includes the fact that Jim and I were *very* well off financially when we became Christians. Well, it wasn't long before Jim decided he wanted to resign from his job and attend seminary so he could go into the ministry. To do this meant we had to sell our *really* nice home and our second car—and move our family of four to a 900-square-foot house.

You wouldn't believe how long the list of "Things This House Didn't Have" was! And the biggies were air-conditioning and a dishwasher (how's that for living in the California desert?). All I can say is it was a really good thing I was learning to pray every day. Well, I took my "Things This House Didn't Have" list and placed it before God in prayer every single day. I prayed right through the list, ticking off each lack on the list. And the next morning and the next I did the same thing again and again—for years!

That's when I developed a saying that helped me through

each day's money trials. My job was to pray daily about my perceived needs. God's job was to meet the "needs" if and when we truly needed them, to meet them in His timing and in His way. Thus my little saying was born: "If God didn't meet it, I didn't need it." Each day I faithfully laid my needs into God's lap through prayer, and each day I was able to rise up from prayer and go about my day without another thought about our finances. They were where they needed to be—in God's hands.

I also took a firm hold onto this translation of Psalm 23:1 (TLB):

> Because the Lord is my Shepherd,
> I have everything I need!

Learning to Be Content

Thank the Lord, I continued to read my Bible for all the decades to come. I'm not sure how else I would have made it through the drastic financial ups and downs our family experienced.

But at some point in this learning-to-pray-about-our-finances process I had found and grabbed onto Philippians 4:11-13 like a woman going down in a stormy sea for the third time. As you read these golden verses, really read them. Note each word and each sentence and each truth. These scriptures are filled with the realities of life. With answers for our struggles. With encouragement. With a mature outlook on having and not having. And with victory.

> [11] ...I have learned in whatever state I am, to be content:

¹² I know how to be abased, and I know how to
abound. Everywhere and in all things I have
learned both to be full and to be hungry, both to
abound and to suffer need.
¹³ I can do all things through Christ who strengthens me.

Grab a pen or pencil and underline "learned." Next, circle
the three couplets that express the extremes of our needs. Then
draw a circle around "content," which signifies the glorious result
of the learning process described in these verses. And finally, if
you haven't already, memorize verse 13, Paul's victory cry.

Having money is not wrong in itself. In fact, money is
amoral—it is neither bad nor good. What makes money bad
or good is our attitude toward it and use of it. Nowhere in the
Bible is being wealthy called a sin. Why, some of the greatest
men of the Old Testament, such as Abraham, Job, and Solomon, were extremely wealthy. And in the New Testament we
read about Joseph of Arimathea, a wealthy leader who followed
Jesus and gave up his own tomb as a burial place for Jesus' body
(Matthew 27:60).

No, money is not the problem. The real issue is how you use
the money you do receive and possess. As with everything you
and your husband have, you are called to be stewards of God's
providential blessing of money. And you are also accountable
to God for how you use it.

Money Is Like a Mirage

Here's an image to keep in mind: Money is like a mirage
in the desert. It gives the appearance of being the answer to all
your problems. But, like that mirage, it is only an illusion. So

for a variety of reasons, you should be concerned about your husband's view and management of money. Here are several key reasons for lifting daily prayers to God for your husband—and you too!

Money does not solve your problems. It is hard as a couple not to think "If-only-we-had-more-money" thoughts all day long every day until the day you die. But here's a fact that is a dose of reality, a real wake-up call: Money does not solve your problems. In fact, it can compound them.

The Bible clearly recognizes that money is necessary for survival. The money you earn and have must be gained honestly and managed carefully. Husbands are to work and provide for their families (1 Timothy 5:8). And the Proverbs 31 woman shows wives multiple ways to contribute to the financial condition of the family.

But God's Word also warns against the misuse of monetary resources. The love of money is referred to as "a root of all kinds of evil" (1 Timothy 6:10). Money can be dangerous because it has the potential to become an instrument that inflames our materialistic desires. It can tempt us to buy what we want, not just what we need.

Money can become a barrier between you and God. When Jesus said, "It is easier for a camel to go through the eye of a needle than for a rich man to enter the kingdom of God" (Mark 10:25), His disciples were stunned. They asked, "Then who can be saved?" (verse 26). This exchange took place after Jesus had confronted a rich young ruler who came to Him desiring to inherit eternal life. Jesus' answer? "Sell whatever you have and give to the poor, and you will have treasure in heaven; and come, take up the cross, and follow Me" (verse 21). Sadly, this wealthy man was unwilling to give up his money. He "went away sorrowful, for he had great possessions" (verse 22).

These words from Jesus speak directly to our hearts all these centuries later, letting us know that money is not the most important thing in our life. Knowing, loving, and following Christ is. You take a lot of pressure off your husband when your first love is Jesus Himself. When this is true in your heart and you are faithful to take your concerns about your financial condition to God in prayer, you will be content with what you have. You will be joyously thankful for all of God's rich blessings. Don't let money matters become a barrier that keeps you and your husband from loving and trusting God and living for Him.

Money is not the measure of your standing with God. In Jesus' day, wealth was seen as a visible sign of a person's spirituality and favor with God. That's why Jesus' disciples were so shocked when He said, "How hard it is for those who have riches to enter the kingdom of God!" (Mark 10:23). They had been taught that wealth was a blessing of God, a reward from Him for being good.

Unfortunately, this misconception is still common in some churches today. The fact some believers enjoy material prosperity is not necessarily an indicator of their spirituality or God's partiality toward them. We are to measure a person's spiritual maturity by their life, not their bank account. The same is true of the lack of wealth. Being poor is not an indicator of God's disapproval or punishment. Wealth is merely one of many ways God blesses His children.

Money can lead to a destructive self-reliance. Money can become a symbol of our accomplishments and efforts, which can lead to pride. There's no doubt our society uses wealth and its outward signs as a measuring stick for success.

But there is great danger in dwelling on what we do have, because it's easy to become proud and reason, "Look what I did!"—or worse, "Why do I need God?" We can slip into living as though all our needs are met with money. If we get sick, no worries! We can afford the finest medical care possible. If my child has a need, no problem! I can pay for a solution.

In Luke 12:16-20, Jesus taught the parable of the rich fool to a crowd so large the people were trampling one another. In this story, the rich man's self-reliance said, "Soul, you have many goods laid up for many years; take your ease; eat, drink, and be merry" (verse 19). Wow, what arrogance—what pride! And how about this man's lifetime goal—lay up money so I can take it easy and eat, drink, and be merry?

Jesus' point is a warning in verse 15: "Take heed and beware of covetousness, for one's life does not consist in the abundance of the things he possesses."

I hope you realize that through Jesus' story about the rich fool we are witnessing God's view on money, riches, and ambition. And knowing what God says about the attitude you should have toward money will help you pray for your husband. You can pray for him to embrace Christ's teachings on possessions and abundance. It will also affect the way *you* approach your needs, desires, wants, and dreams—which will be a positive factor in your husband's life and outlook! Trust God with what you do have. And be a careful manager of those things.

Of course, you will also want to put your trust in God for what you don't have and what you think you need. Again, it comforts me to remember that familiar promise and truth in Psalm 23:1: "The LORD is my shepherd; I shall not want." My friend, God provides everything His children need, or He wouldn't be a good shepherd. You can carry this promise in your heart through better or worse, in poverty or plenty, in sickness and health...till death you do part.

The Joy of Praying for Your Husband

As we look at yet another verse to pray for your husband, don't forget to remind yourself that this verse equally applies to you too. Your thoughts and attitude about money and the use of it are important and can have positive or negative effects on your husband's daily life.

For instance (and I'm speaking of lessons I had to learn the hard way), if you complain about your financial situation or whine and nag about something you wish you had or think you need, or point to what you think is missing in your life, your husband can end up feeling tremendous pressure. You may cause him to think that he's a failure in providing for his family. He might think he needs a second job. He may begin to resent you and stop talking to you. He may think you will never be satisfied and there's no way he can earn your approval.

But if you have a heart that is at rest and content about money, status, and possessions, your husband will be able to relax and rest in the calm you create. He can rejoice and thank God that you make his life bearable, that he can come home each day to a happy wife and a happy home. If you refuse to complain and gripe about worldly goods and needs and wants and wishes and desires, he will lead your family with more confidence.

And I probably don't even need to mention how your failure to curb spending and to help hold down the budget will work directly against his goal of providing for you.

As a wife, I'm sure you can see many reasons why you need to be praying for your husband and how he views money and deals with it. How your husband (and you too!) deals with money is a serious concern. Money is referred to multiple times in the New Testament as "filthy lucre."[1] Just reading or hearing these two words—filthy lucre—makes me want to pray even more fervently that my husband is not obsessed with making money.

And so we pray! Pray and plead with God to help your husband to "seek those things which are above, where Christ is sitting at the right hand of God." Pray that he will "set [his] mind on things above, not on things on the earth" (Colossians 3:1-2). Now look again at the beginning of this chapter and read through our verse to pray.

My Prayer for My Husband
1 Timothy 6:10

Dear Lord, I pray that _____ will not succumb to a love of money that would divert his focus from You and toward all the evils an obsession with money can bring. Give _____ the strength instead to pursue a life of goodness and generosity.

Looking at the Verse

If you read all of 1 Timothy chapter 6, you will discover that verse 10 (the basis for this prayer for your husband) is directed toward those who are teachers. However, as a general principle, it also applies to every believer. This makes verse 10 a perfect scripture to continuously pray for both you and your husband.

Verse 10 begins by informing us that "the love of money is a root of all kinds of evil." Such love is not the only "root" of evil, yet it definitely provides for a lot of evil. But as we considered earlier, it is not money itself that should be the concern for our husbands. Money is neutral. It can be used for good or for evil purposes—depending on the heart and motives of the person who possesses it. What you are to pray for is your husband's attitude toward money. It's the "love of money" that is the sin of greed.

Money has the power to take God's place in your husband's life. It can easily become you and your husband's master. How can you tell if the two of you are becoming "lovers of money"? What are some of the danger signs that indicate you are moving in that direction?

When it comes to praying for your husband, here is a checklist you can pray through.

— Is your husband becoming more concerned with making money?

— Is your husband becoming more worried about money?

— Is your husband becoming more obsessed with wanting more money?

— Is your husband flaunting his money?

— Is your husband stingy with money?

Beyond Prayer, What Can You Do?

Be positive—Are you a positive or negative influence on your husband's attitude toward money? Do you need to stop complaining about what you think you need or don't have and start thanking and praising God for what you do have?

Be watchful—You can't help but stay involved in your husband's life if you are praying for him. After all, you are a couple. As you are praying for the way he handles and deals with money, keep your eyes and heart open, keep the compliments and praise coming—and pray some more!

As his wife, ask questions. It's a key way you can bond with him and be proud of the work he does. You can appreciate—and pray for—the challenges he faces at work. Knowing more about your husband's job makes you a partner with him. You *know*, therefore you can *care*, therefore you *pray*! You are his partner in life, and you can be his silent partner when he is at work.

A loving, concerned wife will pray for her husband to be delivered from temptation and evil (see the Lord's Prayer, Matthew 6:13).

Be aware—Money is a deceptive and hard taskmaster. Spending it can bring a rush of excitement. And everyone loves to see, use, and appreciate what they have purchased. But money cannot ensure health or happiness. Whatever happiness you think your money brings to your life is temporary, an illusion. Only Jesus can give you real happiness each day—and give you eternal life forever. As David mused with regard to being with God, "In Your presence is fullness of joy; at your right hand are pleasures forevermore" (Psalm 16:11).

As wealthy and powerful and successful as David was, his heart's gaze was kept heavenward. Do whatever you must to be sure your focus and devotion are on God.

Be giving—You and your husband are stewards of the resources and money God gives you, and He expects you to manage and

use them wisely, carefully, and thoughtfully—and generously—
no matter how little or much you have. As the Bible says, "Let
each one give as he purposes in his heart, not grudgingly or of
necessity; for God loves a cheerful giver" (2 Corinthians 9:7).
As a couple, pray before you spend, and pray before you give.
Be happy—"cheerful"—when you give!

Be an efficient money manager—Because the management of
your money is in reality a spiritual matter, both you and your
husband are to take your stewardship of God's provision seriously. Discuss and agree on which of you will take care of bill-
paying. Make sure there is regular accountability and setting
of financial goals. Don't become a divorce statistic because you
cannot or will not work together to take care of money problems and agree to manage them as a unit. Be that woman who
"watches over the ways of her household" (Proverbs 31:27).

Be open to financial advice—Unfortunately, our society makes
it all too easy to fall into debt. Credit cards allow us to buy
anything with no thought about how we can pay for it. If you
and your husband are having money problems, get help. I've
seen firsthand how this works. The woman who cuts my hair
and her husband were hopelessly in debt. Thankfully, they got
help. They sought out a financial counselor. Under his guidance,
they built a three-year plan for digging out of debt. Bravo—
they did it! Before they took steps to manage their money more
wisely, they were miserable, and their marriage—and family—
was miserable as well.

Staying out of debt is a daily prayer and practice concern.
Daily prayer and discussion about your financial condition can
keep you and your hubbie on your toes and help you stay out

of debt. It keeps your heads on when it comes to spending and saving. But if you need outside help from an expert, reach out and give it your all.

Check your bank and credit card balances daily. I compare getting into debt to gaining weight. If you don't get on the scales on a regular basis, one day you will wake up and discover you've gained 20 new unwelcome pounds! That can happen with debt as well. If you fail to check your financial status regularly, you will wake up one day hopelessly in debt.

Be a couple whose treasures are in heaven—Money has a powerful place in your marriage. Jesus declared, "Where your treasure is, there your heart will be also" (Matthew 6:21). Money is needed and necessary, but don't let it rule your life and marriage. Remember, you cannot out-give God, and He has promised He will provide. I'm not suggesting that the couple I'm about to introduce is to be the norm, but I do believe we can pray to follow in their footsteps and lay up treasure in heaven:

C.T. Studd was educated at Cambridge, and a hero of the British sport-loving public. In the early 1880s the secular world was shocked by C.T. Studd's deciding upon his conversion to Christ to pursue a missionary career. He had an inheritance of around 29,000 English pounds, which was a sizeable fortune in the 1880s. He gave it all away except for a small amount he gave to his fiancee. Not to be outdone, she gave that money away too. The couple then went to Africa as missionaries with nothing.[2]

A Prayer for When You're Worried About Money

A Prayer from Elizabeth's Heart

Help, Jesus! It's easy to get caught up in the lure of the world around me, to be tempted to amass material possessions, to hoard money. Teach me to seek You and Your kingdom and trust Your provision for my real needs. Help me learn to be content with what You supply. Calm my heart about the future as I count on You to provide in Your perfect timing.[3]

Chapter 7

Praying for Your Husband as He Makes Decisions

If any of you lacks wisdom, let him ask of God, who gives to all liberally and without reproach, and it will be given to him.

JAMES 1:5

With shaking hands and a pained heart, I hit the *end* icon on my cell phone and concluded a life-shattering and life-changing call. The shock was too new for me to register its far-reaching and forever implications. One of my three brothers had just given me the news that our dad, at age 95, had been diagnosed with terminal cancer and would need nursing care for the final days of his life. Our mother was already in another nursing home in the same town with Alzheimer's disease. Our dad had tried to care for her, but she kept wandering off at all hours of the day and night and had no clue who my father and her husband was or who my brothers and I were.

Now we were learning that our father too needed care. My

brothers had all talked and agreed that they could take turns sitting with our dad on the weekends, and maybe "Sister" (that's me!) who didn't have a regular job, could be there during the week until one of them showed up for the weekend vigil. My father's mind was still sharp and none of us wanted him to be alone during his last days. The only issue with their decisions was that I was in California and our dad was in Oklahoma!

Everyone Must Make Decisions

Life requires that you make decisions. And obviously there are a variety of levels of decisions to be made. Some decisions are simple, like which breakfast cereal you will eat for breakfast. Other decisions are a little more complex, like which mobile phone or computer to buy. Still other decisions are even more serious, such as buying a car or a house. Then there are the decisions about whether to homeschool your children or not, whether to change churches or not, whether to undergo chemotherapy or not, or something that is addressed in this book—whether you will submit to your husband or not.

Each and every decision you make, regardless of its level of intensity, can have long-lasting consequences. If you had to make any of these serious decisions on your own, it could create a tremendous amount of stress and anxiety.

But, praise God, He hasn't left you without help! He has given you His Word to show you the way as a lamp to your feet and a light to your path (Psalm 119:105). He has also given you spiritually mature Christians in your church who can help provide guidance. And if you are blessed with seasoned Christian family members, you have a built-in treasure-house of wisdom and love!

I'm assuming because you are reading a book on praying for

your husband that you are a wife. If so, then God has also given you a husband to help you make decisions.

And, by the way, when I was faced with determining whether or not I could leave home to be with my dad every Monday through Friday, I went immediately to Jim so we could talk, pray, and weigh the situation. Amazingly, while I wavered back and forth about being away from Jim, about the money for air travel, and what to do about my commitments, Jim was firm and fully convinced that this was something I needed to do. He said, "Elizabeth, this is a way for you to live out God's admonition to honor your father and mother. You will never regret the time you spend with your parents. Our girls are both married, so you don't need to stay home for them. And I support you in this and will go with you as often as I can get away from work."

Little did we know my father would live—and suffer—for a year. But, as Jim had pointed out in our decision-making process, I have no regrets. And I was able to get on a plane every Monday morning, knowing, *knowing* I had my husband's 100 percent support.

Trusting Your Husband

When you as a wife take your concerns and issues, problems and opportunities to your husband in your decision-making process, you have help, a partner. You have the person who means the most to you and who loves you more than any other person on earth giving his input. Once you have entrusted your husband with helping and guiding you through the process and making the final decision, a great burden will be lifted off your shoulders. You will have peace in your heart and mind with whatever decision the two of you made together.

I know from my mail and interactions with women around

the world that many Christian wives don't trust their husbands or their ability to help make wise decisions. A Christian wife with any spiritual maturity knows what the Bible says about their husband's position as the leader in the home, the marriage, and the family. She also knows that God wants her to submit to her husband's leadership. But for whatever reason, some wives are not sure they can trust their husband's ability to give good, sound advice about any number of decisions she needs to make.

Are you one of these women? Are you a bit hesitant about asking your husband's advice? Are you afraid of what he will say because he is not a Christian—or not a very mature one? Well, by now you know the solution to your hesitancy—and that is prayer. And this next verse will have special meaning for you as you pray for your husband's wisdom in decision-making.

My Prayer for My Husband

James 1:5

Father of all wisdom, I pray that _____ will seek Your wisdom that comes from Your Word so he will make decisions that honor You and bless his family. And Lord, I pray that before _____ makes any decision, he will ask You what he should do. May _____ realize that You are always there for him, ready to supply him with wisdom for every decision he will ever need to make.

This advice and promise from James 1:5 has been helping Christians for centuries! And it can help you and your husband too. The book of James was written to Christians who were scattered because of persecution. James wanted to encourage them in their struggles as they faced trials even as they were reading his letter! He told them how to deal with their trials. And here's some good news—the principles for making any decision are the same, whether it's about how to respond to trials, or about what choice to make in a trying situation.

What can you learn from James 1:5, and how can you use it to pray for your husband?

Pray for your husband to take decision-making seriously—"If any of you lacks wisdom..." Making a right choice should be the top priority when it's time for a decision to be made. The Bible has a special name for a person who thinks he doesn't need help in making decisions: "The way of a *fool* is right in his own eyes, but he who heeds counsel is wise" (Proverbs 12:15).

Asking for and receiving help from God increases the chances you and your husband will make a wise decision. So the first step in praying for your husband is to pray that he understands his need for wisdom and takes it seriously. And while you are praying for him, pray for yourself as well. Pray for wisdom on your part too. You will need wisdom to give your input in a gracious way. Or wisdom to ask questions in a nonthreatening way and with the respect God wants you to exhibit at all times (see Ephesians 5:33). Or wisdom to ask questions about the issue at hand. Or for patience to watch and pray as your man grapples with a solution.

Are you wondering what you can do while you are praying and waiting? Well, it took me some time—and a bushel of failures—but at last I learned a few things to do and not do. Here's a little of what I learned (and please notice the little word *we!*).

— Ask nonthreatening questions to gather information and find out what your husband is thinking—questions like "When would we/you do this?" "When would this happen?" "Do we have the money for this?" "How would we pay for this?"

— Ask questions that point to God's Word. "How can we find out what the Bible says about this?" "Who do we know that can tell us what the Bible says about this?"

— Ask questions that encourage your husband to talk with others about the decision to be made. "Do you know any men you could run this by?" "Are there any men at the church you could run this decision by?"

In time, Jim and I have learned to wait, pray, talk to each other, and talk to others who can give wise advice. You'll see a few other principles we've come up with—and, once again, learned to use after some bad experiences—later in this chapter. But a really big principle is this: When in doubt, don't.

Pray for your husband to respond to God, the ultimate source of help—"...let him ask of God." Your husband probably senses the need for insight specifically on how to make decisions. However, he may be looking to the wrong people for counsel. And the Bible has something to say about this: "He who walks with wise men will be wise, but the companion of fools will be destroyed" (Proverbs 13:20).

Obviously, asking help from God is the channel for finding help. As Jesus instructed His followers, the one who asks receives, who seeks finds, who knocks is blessed (Matthew 7:7-8). Read it for yourself:

Ask, and it will be given to you; seek, and you will find; knock, and it will be opened to you. For

everyone who asks receives, and he who seeks finds,
and to him who knocks it will be opened.

Could it be simpler? Whatever the need, whatever the decision, pray and ask God. Appeal to Him to meet your real needs and give you wisdom and supply what is needed.

How will your husband know what advice God has for him? Part of your continuing prayers for your husband is that he will grow in his knowledge of God's Word. Pray too that he will be involved with the men at your church. As your husband relies on both the collective maturity of others and the instructions he gleans from Scripture, he will increase his chances of making strong, sound decisions.

Pray for your husband to count on God's desire and ability to supply all your needs—"who gives to all liberally." God is the go-to person when you and your husband need help. He is the provider of all wisdom and discernment. And God never tires of hearing your prayers. He never tires of guiding you or giving to you. After all, He is the Good Shepherd. He promises that you shall not want and that He will lead you in the paths of righteousness (Psalm 23:1,3).

In fact, God gives liberally and "generously" (James 1:5 NASB). God's fervency to give to His children in bountiful supply is illustrated in Jesus' teaching as He continues on from Matthew 7:7-8. Note what Jesus added in verses 9-11:

> What man is there among you who, if his son asks
> for bread, will give him a stone? Or if he asks for a
> fish, will he give him a serpent? If you then, being
> evil, know how to give good gifts to your children,
> how much more will your Father who is in heaven
> give good things to those who ask Him!

Jesus assured His followers that if *human* fathers, being evil and sinful, give good things to their children, "how much more" will *God* give to His children who come to Him and ask of Him! And so, we ask...and ask...and ask some more. So pray—today, tomorrow, and every day.

If your husband isn't praying about his decisions, then pray that he will begin to. Pray with every breath that God will move your husband to turn to Him, and will guide your husband toward those who can give wise advice. God can use your prayers to accomplish all this and lead you and your family on the right path.

Another saying that helps me is this: Two wrongs never make a right. So if your husband isn't praying about his decisions (Wrong #1), you do not want to fail to pray (which would be Wrong #2). And so you pray, no matter what. And you keep on praying—asking, seeking, and knocking—believing God's promise that you will receive, find, and God will open the door to your husband's heart.

We've covered some ways you can talk with your husband and some questions you can ask about the decisions that he must make (or will make). Again, burn into your heart the fact that two wrongs never make a right. Your husband's neglect or failure to try to make wise decisions regarding you and your family is Wrong #1. But if you blow up, lose it, scream, yell, have a fit, and belittle or berate your husband, that is definitely Wrong #2.

Your goal in your interactions with your husband comes from God's Word: You are to "walk in the Spirit" so you produce the fruit of love, patience, kindness, and self-control (Galatians 5:16,22-23).

And here's another goal: Follow in the steps of God's ideal woman and wife as pictured in the Proverbs 31 woman: "She opens her mouth with wisdom, and on her tongue is the law of kindness" (verse 26).

It's sobering to think that our prayers are hindered when we fail to walk in the Spirit and instead, we choose to sin. God's fervency to give the wisdom your husband needs is related to the fervency of your prayers for your husband. To repeat, as James wrote, "The effective, fervent prayer of a righteous [wife] avails much" (James 5:16).

Pray for your husband to count on God's help—"...without reproach." In answer to your or your husband's prayers, God gives to you "without reproach" or "without finding fault" (NIV). As many times as you and your husband want to ask God for wisdom, you will never find God tapping His divine finger and saying, "You again! What did you do with the wisdom I gave you last time? When will you ever learn? When are you going to get it? What's wrong with you?"

God isn't going to give you or your husband a rap across the knuckles for daring to ask Him for wisdom to make good decisions. Your heavenly Father is not stingy. Nor does He belittle you for imposing on His goodness. And, as we've noticed, this verse from James 1:5 is God's admonition that you do just that! You have His full support for your prayers for wisdom.

James essentially said the same thing in James 1:5. Let's review it, and note especially the final line:

> If any of you lacks wisdom,
> let him ask of God, who gives to all liberally
> and without reproach, and it will be given to him.

Here, James gives further affirmation of God's support. He encourages prayer, assuring us that when wisdom is needed and you or your husband pray, "it will be given to him."

Yet even with all these assurances that God's wisdom is indeed available to us, we still make plenty of blunders in our decision making. See for yourself how even great men of the Bible made a few bad decisions. You may even want to take notes!

Famous Decision-Making Blunders from the Bible

Can you imagine your husband waking up tomorrow morning, stretching, and saying, "Let's see...how many wrong decisions can I make today?" Or, "How many choices can I make today that will do harm to me or my wife and family?" Or, "How many decisions can I make today that will dishonor God and be a personal affront to His holiness?"

And yet, in many cases, that's essentially what happens when your husband (and don't forget yourself!) doesn't take his decision making seriously, or he makes decisions without even thinking or asking advice of anyone. And especially when he doesn't take his options to God through prayer and searching His Word.

The Bible shows us many examples of men who made poor decisions. Do you think God is trying to tell husbands something? As you look at the consequences of these bad decisions, may you find yourself strengthened in your resolve to pray for your husband.

Abraham. This "father of the Jewish nation" asked his wife, Sarah, to lie about their marital status. Why? He was afraid. In *fear,* he asked Sarah, "Please say you are my sister, that it may be well with me for your sake, and that I may live because of you" (Genesis 12:13). A great tragedy was averted as God intervened to keep the men of Egypt away from Sarah.

Lot. Abraham's nephew, Lot, was asked to choose between the grassy land of the Jordan valley and the drier hill country to pasture his cattle. The commonsense choice was obvious—pick the well-watered valley, right? Wrong! That valley and its wicked cities of Sodom and Gomorrah ultimately corrupted Lot's family. In the end, Lot's decision made from *greed* caused him to lose all his possessions, his wife, and the respect and morality of his two daughters. These consequences added up to a sky-high price paid for one wrong decision (see Genesis 13:10-13; 19).

Moses. God's chosen leader, Moses, made several blunders in decision making. The first came while he was still a prince in Egypt. It was made out of *pride*. Moses, thinking God wanted him to be the leader of the Jewish people, took matters into his own hands and killed an Egyptian (Exodus 2:11-15). True, eventually that would be God's decision for Moses...but in God's timing it wouldn't happen for another 40 years!

The second blunder came while Moses was leading two million thirsty people through the desert during a 40-year trek. He was commanded by God to "speak to the rock before their eyes, and it will yield its water; thus you shall bring water for them out of the rock" (Numbers 20:8). However, out of anger over the rebellious and complaining attitude of the people, Moses chose to strike the rock—not just once, but twice (verses 10-11). That wrong decision made in *anger* cost Moses the privilege of going into the Promised Land (verse 12).

David. This second king of Israel chose to commit adultery—a decision made from *lust*. Then when he couldn't cover up his sin, he chose to murder the husband of Bathsheba, the woman he lusted after (2 Samuel 11).

I'm sure you are seeing the picture in full color. A single wrong decision can lead to sin and change the course of your life forever, and that is true of your husband as well. The decisions these men made were based on fear, greed, anger, and lust.

A Few Words of Advice

As Jim and I look back, we realize we learned many times the hard way that, when we didn't pray, or consult with each other, or seek God's wisdom, or ask for godly advice, we just about always made bad, wrong, or lesser decisions. So, speaking from personal experience, I want to give you a handful of guiding principles for making decisions. These principles have become personal slogans Jim and I use to remind ourselves to pray *before* we make decisions.

— No decision made without prayer (Philippians 4:6-7).

— When in doubt, don't (Romans 14:23).

— Always ask "What does the Bible say?" (John 17:17).

— Always do what you know is right (James 4:14).

— Don't let fear influence you (1 John 4:18).

Doing Your Part Through Prayer

Those biblical illustrations are sobering, aren't they? We are just as capable of making the same kinds of wrong decisions as many others have made down through time. In fact, we have probably already made some really bad choices! But that doesn't mean all is lost. You can assist your husband—and yourself!—in this area of making better decisions. How?

Pray, thanking God for His forgiveness. If you are a believer like David and all others who have sinned and made bad decisions,

God's grace is sufficient. In 1 John 1:9, God tells us exactly what to do after we fail: "If we confess our sins, He is faithful and just to forgive us our sins and to cleanse us from all unrighteousness." God knows you and your husband are sinners saved by His grace. He isn't asking the two of you to be perfect, just progressing. Learn from each wrong decision, and pray for wisdom not to make the same ones again.

Pray for your husband to check his motives. It's very insightful when you and your husband analyze what is prompting you as you make your next decision. That decision is not being made in a vacuum. There is always something that is propelling you or your husband to want to do what you want to do.

Pray for your husband to seek wisdom from the Bible. Once again, pray for your husband to get into the habit of asking, "What does the Bible say about this decision we must make or are about to make?" Pray that he embraces the Bible as his standard for his decisions.

Pray for your husband to find some wise mentors and counselors. Wisdom is contagious. If your husband spends time with mature Christian men, he will be exposed to their good examples. He will be set with a corps of counselors who can help him—"for by wise counsel you will wage your own war, and in a multitude of counselors there is safety" (Proverbs 24:6).

Pray for your husband to develop patience. I don't know about you, but when I make quick, hurried, or forced decisions, they usually turn out to be bad ones. This is where prayer comes to your and your husband's rescue. How? Prayer makes you wait. It slows you down. It puts on the brakes. Patience in prayer also allows time for truths and options to surface as you move toward a decision. Prayer acknowledges your dependence on God and reminds you of His power and provision, along with His willingness to provide the wisdom you need. Prayer reveals motives as God searches your heart. Prayer will reveal if you or your husband are making a decision based on worldliness, peer pressure, fear, greed, or laziness.

A Prayer to Pray from the Heart of Paul

Ephesians 1:15-17

I...do not cease to give thanks for you,
making mention of you in my prayers:
that the God of our Lord Jesus Christ,
the Father of glory,
may give to you the spirit of wisdom and
revelation in the knowledge of Him.

Chapter 8

Praying for Your Husband's Health

*Do you not know that your body is the temple of
the Holy Spirit who is in you, whom you have
from God, and you are not your own? For you
were bought at a price; therefore glorify God in
your body and in your spirit, which are God's.*

1 CORINTHIANS 6:19-20

What thoughts might run through your mind when,
at 35,000 feet, the person sitting next to you on
the airplane starts convulsing? Unfortunately, I can answer that
question. Regardless of who that person is, you fight down your
panic, and frantically push and push...and push the flight attendant button and rally those nearby to get some help! You wonder, *Where are those flight attendants when you need one?* And then
you realize only two seconds have gone by! To make matters even
more desperate, the person next to you is your husband! Talk
about a guaranteed way to ruin the end of a vacation—which up
until this moment had been absolutely perfect!

117

Well, needless to say, I was a wreck on the inside. I did what I had to do—only by the grace of God. Any strength, control, and clarity of mind I possessed was drawn solely from God's abundant grace. Jim's episode didn't last long, and an attendant did arrive right away, and, praise God, my husband seemed okay after coming out of his convulsion.

Thankfully, my story has a happy ending. No, Jim didn't have an epileptic seizure. And no, he didn't have a heart attack. After finally convincing the flight crew that ordering a wheelchair and an ambulance was not necessary when we landed, we slowly walked to the next gate and took our final flight home. (Oh, thank You, Lord, for home sweet home!)

However, in the months that followed and many medical tests later, it was determined that Jim's heart was slowly ticking down. He needed a pacemaker that would help supply a tiny jolt every time his heart wanted to slow down too much. This little jolt would cause less blood to be sent to the brain, which was the cause of the convulsions he had on the airplane.

Every wife who has been married for any length of time faces or will face an experience similar to mine. Hopefully it will not occur on an airplane! Worry, unfortunately, seems to be one of the top time-honored ways we wives deal with our husbands' health issues. As I have talked with women the world over, I would have to say health issues are at or near the top of most wives' List of Concerns for their husbands, including my own.

But there are seasons with little or no worry over health. If you are a younger married couple, you and your husband may seem invincible. Praise God for your young adult lives and health! Please enjoy every minute of such carefree vitality and unending energy. I smile every time I recall the glorious days when Jim and I had seemingly unlimited energy and abilities. We camped and sailed, water-skied and even snow-skied once in a while. We were hikers and runners too. One year, Jim led a group of seminary students to Israel and, rather than take the tram to the top of Masada (which, in Hebrew, means "fortress"), the two of us walked all 1300 of those feet straight up the mountain. Oh, and as newlyweds we took the stairs to the top of the Washington Monument in Washington, DC so we wouldn't have to pay the 25-cent fee for taking the elevator. (I'm not sure I'm so proud of that decision!)

But with the passage of time, real and potential health problems will begin to creep into the picture. Time and birthdays flying by will become periodic wake-up calls to begin paying better attention to your health. Then it will be time to sober up and do something about any bad habits that are having negative effects on your body and lifestyle.

You Have Two Options

As I recall Jim's situation and think on all the health scares and issues wives might have to grapple with when it comes to their husbands' health, I see two options: Either we can worry, or we can pray. And isn't that what we have been talking about so far in this book!

Even if you are praying more and worrying less, that doesn't mean you aren't concerned about your husband. In fact, as we are stressing in this book on praying for your sweet husband, you are so concerned that you are going to the highest possible authority to make your appeal—to your all-powerful, almighty heavenly Father, the Great Physician, the One who cares the most for you and your husband.

And here's another principle: You can worry about your husband's health, or you can do something physically about it. You can do your part! You can do what you can do. There's no need to nag. Just quietly—and prayerfully—place his health at the top of your to-do list. Roll up your sleeves and work some dietary magic!

Obviously, there are many practical things you can do as a wife to contribute to your husband's health. You can make sure the foods he eats at home are healthy. You can plan and prepare meals, snacks, and lunches that energize him for his work without unwanted calories and unhealthful ingredients. You can stock snack foods that are good for your family. You can also work together as a couple to participate in some kind of exercise.

I'm sure none of this is news to you, but as a wife who cares more about your husband than any other person on earth does, you can decide to be proactive. You can read and study up on health. You can talk to others who know more about nutrition than you do. You can even take cooking classes that teach you new or better ways to cook for health. You can create grocery lists that have your husband's heart, weight, muscles, and health in mind.

God Is Concerned About Every Area of Your Life

In the Bible, there are many pages and scriptures that address health and healthy living. For instance, immediately after the children of Israel escaped Egypt, God instructed Moses about establishing the priesthood and worship for the people (Leviticus 1–10). Then in the next five chapters (11–15) we read of God's concern for the health, hygiene, and diet of His people.

It's obvious some of God's regulations were intended to mark the Israelites as being different from the pagans and wicked people who surrounded them. Nevertheless, these laws and regulations were also given for the people's health and protection. God's guidelines and restrictions on food consumption helped the Israelites to avoid diseases that were serious threats in that time and place. Although the people themselves didn't understand medically why God's restrictions were given, their obedience made them healthier and, in many cases, kept them alive.

God was extremely exacting as He minutely described how to identify and diagnose infections and skin diseases like leprosy and how to keep them from spreading. He instructed the Israelites regarding which foods to eat and which to avoid. Long before anyone knew about the harmfulness of eating uncooked meats, God laid out regulations and instructions for properly cooking food.

God gave as much instruction regarding health as He did concerning the priesthood and worship. Why would He do that? Because God is interested in the whole person. He is concerned about the physical as well as the spiritual and moral health of His people.

Pray with an Eternal Perspective

Like God's care for Israel's well-being, we too need to care for and watch over our physical health. And, like God, we also need to view our health with an eternal perspective.

Think about this: Did you realize that Christians are "fellow citizens with the saints and members of the household of God" (Ephesians 2:19)? With this citizenship should come a realization that this world is not our home. We are strangers, sojourners, pilgrims, and foreigners (1 Peter 2:11) who "eagerly wait for the Savior, the Lord Jesus Christ" (Philippians 3:20).

So in one sense, our physical health, even though it is a concern, is really a secondary concern. This doesn't mean we shouldn't pray for the physical health of others, especially our husbands. But it does mean we are to pay more attention to developing an eternal perspective. We are to pray beyond physical issues and "seek those things which are above, where Christ is, sitting at the right hand of God. Set your mind on things above, not on things on the earth" (Colossians 3:1-2).

One place we are given a clue as to how we should approach the issue of praying for the health for our husbands is found in 3 John 2. The apostle John wrote, "Beloved, I pray that you may prosper in all things and be in health, just as your soul prospers." John knew of the excellent nature of his dear friend Gaius, and therefore he was praying that Gaius's physical health would match his spiritual vitality. With God's heavenly and spiritual perspective in mind, here is the scripture and a prayer that will help you keep this balance as you pray. Take a minute to read the verses at the beginning of this chapter—use these verses to lift up a prayer for your husband's health.

My Prayer for My Husband
1 Corinthians 6:19-20

Father, I pray that _____ will understand that his body is Your temple and that the Holy Spirit now lives within him. Help _____ realize what a great price was paid for this personal relationship with You. Work in _____'s heart and life. Cause him to desire to make every effort to honor You with his body.

Unpacking the Verse—What Does It Mean?

As you read through these verses, realize they are a call to holy living. The Christians in Corinth were living in a truly awful place. The city and its worship centered around the Temple of Aphrodite, the Greek goddess of love. This temple had more than 1000 priestesses who were in actuality "religious" prostitutes. It's no wonder this city was so morally corrupt that its very name became synonymous with debauchery and moral depravity.

But there's good news! Paul wrote this letter to the Corinthians to convince Christians of their need to assume a different mind-set and the reasons they should live a different lifestyle than those around them. What Paul wrote to these believers translates into principles you can pray for your husband—and, of course, for yourself!

The function of your husband's body—"Your body is the temple." In the Old Testament, the presence of God first dwelled in the tabernacle and later in Solomon's temple. Jews came from all over the known world to worship God at the temple. Just as Old Testament worshipers were to approach the temple with honor and respect, Paul wrote his readers to inform them that as believers, they were to honor and respect their body, in which Christ's Spirit resided. He began by asking, "Do you not know your body is the temple...?"

As a believer in Christ, your husband's body is the special dwelling place of God. Therefore, you should be praying that your husband will desire to do whatever is necessary to take care of his body—which is God's temple.

The occupant of your husband's body—"Your body is the temple of the Holy Spirit who is in you, whom you have from God." Here, Paul's emphasis is on the indwelling Holy Spirit: He is in you and is a gift from God. Like salvation, the power of the Holy Spirit is needed for living the Christian life and is a gift of God.

And so you pray, certainly for yourself, but also for your

dearly beloved. As you pray, ask God to cause your husband to realize and understand that *his* body is the temple of the Holy Spirit, that the Holy Spirit resides in *him,* and that *he* must yield himself to the Spirit so the Spirit can work in *him.*

And here's something to note: The context of 1 Corinthians 6:15-18 is in reference to sexual sin. When you pray about your husband's body as being the temple of the Holy Spirit, you are praying that he will resist sexual temptation as well as the temptation to abuse his body with overeating, chemical abuse, and even excessive stressing over his job.

The owner of your husband's body—"...you are not your own? For you were bought at a price." Here Paul painted a word picture that came from the practice of buying and selling people in a slave market. Paul referred to Christ Himself purchasing us out of the slave market of sin with His death on the cross!

When (and if) your husband accepted Christ, whether he realizes it or not, he relinquished all personal rights to his body. His body was purchased with the death of Christ, and now belongs to Him. Paul expressed this truth in this way: "I have been crucified with Christ; it is no longer I who live, but Christ lives in me; and the life which I now live in the flesh I live by faith in the Son of God, who loved me and gave Himself for me" (Galatians 2:20). This, my praying friend, is what you are diligently praying for your husband.

The purpose of your husband's body—"Glorify God in your body." This is stated as an urgent command, not an option. Your husband's willingness to do his part fulfills the supreme purpose for his existence—to glorify God. This isn't the only time in this book you will pray verses that center on God's desire that your husband's actions would glorify Him. Here, with these verses, you are asking God to work in your husband's life in ways that bring honor to the person of God, who alone is worthy of your husband's obedience and adoration.

Praying for Your Husband's Health

Now that you and I have a better understanding of what these verses imply, we can better pray for our husbands. As I am reading through these verses in 1 Corinthians 6:19-20, I'm applying them to both Jim and me: Our bodies both as husband and wife belong to God and are to be kept pure, managed, and used for God, not for ourselves. Our physical bodies are meant for service, not for sin.

And so I'm praying not only for Jim, but for myself as well—and you would do the same for your husband and yourself.

Yes, it's a fact that our flesh is corrupt with sin and is a battleground of the spiritual life. But with the indwelling Holy Spirit, your husband's body can be a beautiful instrument of righteousness.

Are you wondering, *How can this be? How can it happen? And what can I do to help make it happen?* Ultimately it is the indwelling Holy Spirit's job to sanctify our husbands, to make them aware of sin and be more sensitive to it. This means it is not our job, as wives, to cause or make our husbands grow spiritually and watch over temptation on all fronts. But it *is* our job and privilege to do our part by praying always, constantly, frequently, fervently, at all times, and without ceasing.[1]

Here's some help on how you can pray for your husband's body and his battles:

Pray for your husband's physical health—Paul declared, "I discipline my body and bring it into subjection, lest...I myself should become disqualified" (1 Corinthians 9:27). Paul's discipline was a goal—he wanted to please God. He knew that if he was disqualified physically, it would affect his life and ministry.

Physical discipline means eating sensibly, choosing healthy foods, and watching how the food we consume affects our energy (and even our waistline!). It also means exercising for health and stamina. As Paul wrote to Timothy, "Bodily exercise profits a little" (1 Timothy 4:8). I like what George Müller said: "I cannot take care of my soul, God can keep that; but my body is for me to take care of."[2]

As your husband's wife, you cannot watch over ever bite of food your husband puts into his mouth. And you cannot be his personal trainer. But you can watch your own weight, put healthy meals on the table, and even suggest you both take a walk around the neighborhood in the evenings. And if you have children, take them with you! It will be great family fun.

Pray for your husband's spiritual health—At first glance you might be wondering how praying for your husband's *spiritual* health affects his *physical* body. Obviously, you are to pray for your husband to resist temptation, which is a spiritual discipline. And you are to pray that he will read and study his Bible, which is also a spiritual discipline.

It also helps to remember the fruit of the Spirit includes "self-control" (Galatians 5:23). This means that as you are praying for your husband's spiritual discipline, you could be praying that he would say *no* to that second or third donut!

There is an additional element of spiritual discipline that is often forgotten: You need to pray that when your husband sins, he will be quick to acknowledge it. The confession of sin is another spiritual discipline that is vital to your husband's well-being. The Bible is laced with examples of the physical body being affected due to a failure to admit sin. Read along as David gives a vivid testimonial of what happened to his body when he failed to acknowledge his sin:

When I kept silent, my bones grew old through my
groaning all the day long. For day and night Your
hand was heavy upon me; my vitality was turned
into the drought of summer (Psalm 32:3-4).

Now notice David's willful decision to confess his sin to God:

I acknowledged my sin to You, and my iniquity I
have not hidden. I said, "I will confess my transgression to the LORD," and You forgave the iniquity of my sin (verse 5).

And the result? Notice the change in David's heart and
language after he said, "I will confess my transgression to the
LORD."

Be glad in the LORD and rejoice, you righteous; and
shout for joy, all you upright in heart! (verse 11).

And so you pray! Pray a prayer expressing your commitment
to God to become a prayer warrior on behalf of your husband.
I personally wrote out a commitment to God as well. And pray
for more physical and spiritual discipline in both of you. Watching over your health and making changes in your daily life will
give you a greater measure of the physical vitality that fuels the
spiritual life—and the plan God has in mind for each of you.
What glory that will be!

Beyond Prayer, What Can You Do?

Be a positive influence. It's scary—and good—that you and I as
wives can either be a positive or negative influence on our spouses
when it comes to health. So pray. Pray to be a positive influence.

And you don't have to make a scene or big to-do—or even say one word!—to make a difference. Without a word you can use self-control when it comes to your own eating habits. Without a word you can help your husband with a weight problem by choosing not to tempt him with a kitchen full of junk food. Without a word—and with a little effort—you can set meals on the table so you can eat at home as much as possible. You'll save lots of money and, at the same time, control the types and portions of food you both eat.

Be a pray-er, not a worrier. I'll probably say this more than once in this book, but it's worth repeating. You can worry, which usually expresses itself in nagging, hovering, or mothering your husband about his eating habits and lack of exercise.

Or you can pray. And a good time to pray prayers for health is when breakfast, lunch, and dinnertime roll around. This doesn't mean you can't do your part to be a helper to your guy (see Genesis 2:18), but like the other areas in which you are praying for your husband, ultimately you must place your husband's health into God's hands.

A Word from the Heart of Paul to Pray
Philippians 4:6-7

Be anxious for nothing, but in everything by prayer
and supplication, with thanksgiving, let your
requests be made known to God; and the peace
of God, which surpasses all understanding, will
guard your hearts and minds through Christ Jesus.

Chapter 9

Praying for Your Husband's Use of Time

*See then that you walk circumspectly, not as
fools but as wise, redeeming the time, because
the days are evil. Therefore do not be unwise,
but understand what the will of the Lord is.*

EPHESIANS 5:15-17

As a busy woman, your natural tendency at the sound of the alarm each morning is probably to hit the floor running (like I do!). And for many women, each day also includes hitting the road at some point as you head off to a job, or get the kids to school, or run those 1001 errands. At the first sound of the alarm (or of a crying baby!), you are often tempted to groan, "Oh, no—not another day. I have so much to do! I'll never get it all done." The blare of your alarm reminds you (once again, just in case you could ever forget) that you are faced with a life filled and overflowing with responsibilities and a shortage of time to make it all happen.

Well, if it's any encouragement to you, most everyone is faced with the same dilemma when they start each day. They too have only 24 hours, 1440 minutes, or 86,400 seconds in each of their days. And they too are laden with a lot that needs to get done before the day is over.

Time. It's like nothing else. You can't create more of it. You can't store it up. You can't retrieve it. Once time passes, it's gone forever. God created time, which means every created being is subject to that time. Only God exists outside of time.

So how can you—and your husband—get more time? Because the two of you are a couple, I can think of only two sure ways to get more time:

- First, you can pray and pay greater attention to *your use of time,* and work at becoming a better time manager.

- And second, you can pray for *your husband's use of his time,* and that he will work at becoming a better time manager.

After all, there are two of you, and you will either work *with* each other or *against* each other, depending on how each of you views and deals with time.

So, are you wondering, *How does praying for my husband and his time help me with my time?* I'm so glad you asked!

Praying for Your Husband's Time

Because you and your husband as "one flesh" are a team, ideally the two of you have the potential to accomplish twice as much by working together toward common goals, or goals the two of you have set for yourselves. Isn't that what Solomon suggested in Ecclesiastes 4:9? He wrote, "Two are better than one, because they have a good reward for their labor."

You will notice I said "ideally." Unfortunately, we live in an imperfect world, and maybe the two of you are not acting as one. Maybe it looks like one of you isn't shouldering their share of the burden—or is pulling in the opposite direction, toward an opposing goal.

These conflicting purposes can be counterproductive and cause you to feel like you are buried under a pile with no way out and no one to help you. Managing so much responsibility without help can cause you to be anxious, or give up, or become resentful toward your husband. You get to the point where you simply cannot see how you are ever going to dig yourself out from under so many obligations, especially without the help of your husband. Maybe you find yourself thinking, *If only I could have my husband pitch in and lend me a few of his hours, minutes, seconds, and muscle to finish the priority items that are on my plate today!*

With that in mind, you have some choices to make. You can nag, throw a tantrum, harden your heart, resent your husband...or you can pray for your husband's understanding and his use of his time, not just to assist you, but to move toward fulfilling the purposes God has for him and also make a greater contribution in the world.

As a wife who wants to do all to the glory of God, you must rule out and get rid of any negative, fleshly responses and instead, pray. When you do this, you are putting your problem in the right place—right into God's hands. And while you are praying for your husband, take the next step and ask God for His help for yourself—that you would become a better time manager, even an excellent one!

Praying for Your Husband's Use of Time

Before we dive into this next prayer drawn from Ephesians 5:15-16, be sure to read these verses in your Bible. Or you can read the verses on the first page of this chapter.

As you read on, keep in mind that the message in these two verses originated back to Paul's appeal to believers in Christ to "be imitators of God as dear children" (verse 1). You and your husband have a lofty calling to live and act in a godly manner. And to imitate and reflect God, you are to "walk" and live in a way that pleases Him. And, of course, you'll want to pray for your husband to also walk wisely.

My Prayer for My Husband
Ephesians 5:15-17

Eternal Father of all time, I pray that _____ will look carefully at his day and make wise use of his time. Your Word says this world is evil and offers opportunities for making foolish decisions just about every single minute!

Lord, You have given _____ and me this one precious day. Guide _____ and me to understand together what Your will is for us right now, today.

Now, what is involved in wise living? And how does it affect your husband's use of his time? And what difference does the use of time make anyway?

Wise living saves time—"See then that you walk circumspectly, not as fools but as wise" (verse 15). "Circumspectly" means being careful, exacting, and sensible. When we are careful and have a reason for what we do and don't do—and how we do and don't spend our time—we make fewer mistakes and waste less time, which saves time and gets more work done!

I know all about this principle. Unfortunately I learned it the hard way. As a young mother with two little girls born thirteen months apart, my hands were full. There was always a mess to clean up, a squabble to settle, another load of laundry to take care of. I ran myself ragged every day—and fell into bed half dead each night.

Then the glorious day arrived when both girls were in school. Yippee—I was free! At last I could sit with my feet up and actually enjoy a cup of hot chocolate—and watch the morning talk shows, read for hours, take a nap—or two. Then, oops—I almost forgot! It was time to rush and pick up the girls from school, go get some groceries, hurry in the door, and slap together an evening meal for when Jim got home. Too bad I forgot to scurry back and make the bed before everyone came home!

I was the "fool" or the "unwise" person who squandered my time away. I spent it without discipline. I passed through days and weeks without a plan—and with little or nothing to show for my efforts. I never thought of spending some of my time praying for those at church who were suffering. I could have signed up to make and take meals to new mothers or someone going through cancer treatments who needed special foods. I could have driven elderly folks to their doctor appointments. I could have even worked on some life goals, if I'd had any! On and on the list of "could haves" went.

But praise be to God, He brought a mentor my way who was a time management expert. Using scriptures, practical tips, and sharing what she had learned, my heart got turned around until every minute became viewed as a gift from God—and a stewardship. I grew to value time, to carefully schedule and appropriate it, to operate on a schedule based on priorities, hopefully God's priorities. In short, I learned to walk circumspectly, not as a fool but as a wise woman.

In our marriage, my husband always has been and still is the master time manager. He was known and good-naturedly teased by our church staff because he never went anywhere without his two-inch-thick planner. Not only did he run our home and family and finances out of that magic notebook, but he kept watch over his many ministry responsibilities.

I'm hoping this is true of your husband, that he is already aware of time and is learning the best ways to use it. If not, well, you know what to do—pray!

Wise living redeems time—"...redeeming the time" (verse 16). Wise living also involves redeeming the time. To redeem time means to buy it back by putting it to good use whenever there's an opportunity. In these verses the apostle Paul points out that the days are evil. But with the wise use of our time, we can use it to accomplish good.

When you and your husband are careful to reject foolish or unwise behavior with all its vanities, you are buying back time that can then be used to fulfill God's priorities at home and at work—that is, do the work of God. I like the way this Bible translation words the passage we are focusing on in this chapter:

> Be careful how you act; these are difficult days.
> Don't be fools; be wise: make the most of every
> opportunity you have for doing good. Don't act
> thoughtlessly, but try to find out and do whatever
> the Lord wants you to (Ephesians 5:15-17 TLB).

Wise living recognizes the purpose of time—"Therefore do not be unwise, but understand what the will of the Lord is" (verse 17). How much time could you and your husband save if you always did exactly what God wanted you to do? Just think how much time you waste daily in forgetting appointments and commitments, in backtracking or starting over, or having to scrap everything and go in another direction. Knowing God's will and choosing to do it produces perfect timing and time management, with no wasted effort.

Doing God's Will

And there it is! The secret to *redeeming time* or *buying back time* or *making the most of every opportunity* is knowing and doing God's will. And what may that be? God's direction is always found in the Bible. His plans for you and your husband unfold as you read and study His Word, apply it, and pray for wisdom. When you seek to do His will, the management of your minutes, hours, days, and years will come much easier and be more productive.

All of this is yours because you are seeking to travel in God's direction, toward His will. Instead of struggling against God and His plans and purposes for you, you pray daily for God's guidance and wisdom to do His work His way.

Two Types of Husbands

Praise God, His will is not some big mystery. No, it's usually the thing right in front of you. His will involves doing your part in your roles and responsibilities as a wife and mother. To accomplish God's will, you need to understand about planning, and so does your husband. When using time well, there are two types of husbands. Both types need your daily prayers.

The Type 1 Husband—This is the kind of man many women are married to. This man doesn't think about his day the night before...or when he gets up...or at any time during the day. Bless his heart, he just goes with the flow. He doesn't have any big plans for today or any day other than to show up at work and do his job. Beyond what occurs at his job, he drifts through life, doing whatever comes up or whatever he feels like doing, even if that's doing nothing.

If this describes your spouse, he needs you to pray a prayer like we have in this chapter, "My Prayer for My Husband." Pray for God to make him aware of the importance of time and using that time for good purposes—for God's will.

The Type 2 Husband—This is the man you are praying for your husband to become. This husband plans ahead. Planning is a discipline and a lifestyle for him. He has lists, schedules, and goals, and he is producing results! You might call him a driven man. Well, that's the good news!

Now, the bad news is that sometimes when this type of husband fixates on his physical plans, he can end up neglecting the spiritual and personal parts of his life. He doesn't plan to neglect his relationship with God or his family. Rather, that's just not where his focus is.

So you know what to do, right? Pray! Pray that his plans include time for God, time with Christian men, and time with his family. Thank God for your husband's commitment to his work and to providing for his family. But pray that he will understand that God and family are priorities that really matter. Pray that your wonderful husband will "seek first the kingdom of God and His righteousness," being confident that when he puts God first, "all these things"—his plans and goals and roles—"shall be added" (Matthew 6:33).

Principles for Planning

So one type of husband doesn't plan, but maybe with prayer on your part and maybe some help from some of the men in your church, he will want to adopt some of these principles. For others who are planners, these principles may be more for your benefit. But if your husband is interested in learning more about planning and other marks of leadership, my husband, Jim, has written the book *A Leader After God's Own Heart*. Right now, I want to share a few thoughts from a chapter in Jim's book, which is entitled "Planning...Brings Focus to Your Leadership." [1]

As you start to read about planning, think about the following well-known saying, and remember it each day. And share it with your husband too:

> If you don't plan your day,
> someone else will be glad to plan it for you!

Planning involves a partnership with God—Planning begins by praying. The success of any day for you or your husband begins with being fully dependent upon God for everything that will or might happen in your day.

Planning involves people—In order for you and your husband to get the most out of your day, involve each other in the planning. What can you do to help your husband's day go easier? Does he need clothes picked up from the dry cleaner? What can he do to ease your day? Maybe he can pick up the kids after soccer practice on his way home from work. And speaking of kids, don't forget to involve them in helping with household chores (as in, plan them in!). Enlisting the help of others is not using them, it's involving them!

Planning involves a plan—How can you plan without a strategy? You need a Plan A. Good planning starts the night before when you think ahead to the next day. That will allow you to wake up with Plan A all set to go. But if something changes or comes up, you quickly move to Plan B. You still have a plan in play. It's just not the one you started with in the morning or even the night before.

Planning involves planned neglect—You and your husband cannot do everything today, but you can do some things. Plan in priority order, and plan to neglect everything that isn't on that list and transfer it to another day's list.

Some time ago I clipped a newspaper article about a famous concert pianist who was asked, "What is the secret of your success?"

His summed up his answer in two words: "Planned neglect!"

When asked for clarification, he described what he did when he first began to study the piano. He was young, and many things were demanding his time and attention. After he took care of each demand, he would return to his music—until another activity arose. Eventually it occurred to him that he was giving his music the leftovers of his time. It was taking second place to any little thing that happened to distract him. Finally he made the decision to deliberately neglect everything else until his practice time was completed. That program of planned neglect gave him back the eight hours a day he needed to practice and accounted for his success.

The principle of "planned neglect" is the same for you and your husband. You cannot do everything. In fact, you cannot do most things. But you can—and must—plan to neglect nonpriority things so you can do well on those few things that are the most important.

Redeeming Time Together

As a couple, you and your hubby are a "package deal," a team. God intended for you to produce a greater impact together than you could do separately. Granted, most couples, at some time in their marriages, are not on the same page when it comes to redeeming time and using it wisely. So remember: No preaching. No nagging. No lecturing. Instead, put your time, energy, and emotions into praying for your husband's use of time. And while you are praying, ask God for the wisdom and grace to handle your expectations and disappointments well.

Here are some principles to guide you as you pray for and hopefully with your husband:

You redeem time when you... make the most of your marriage day by day. Every bride has dreamed of how her marriage would be, could be, should be, or might be. And sure enough, every bride has dozens of wake-up calls when she must face the fact that her expectations have not been realized. So what's a wife to do?

Rather than waste time in regret, sorrow, or anger, reorder your priorities according to God's will for you as a wife. Focus on what you can do, and refuse to dwell on what your husband is or isn't doing. Get back to the basics of praying. If things aren't right, start praying for God to make them right, beginning with you and your heart. We learn this from Jesus as He talked with a group He addressed as hypocrites because they thought they were better than others:

> Judge not, that you be not judged...And why do you look at the speck in your brother's eye, but do not consider the plank in your own eye? Or how can you say to your brother, "Let me remove the speck

from your eye"; and look, a plank is in your own eye? Hypocrite! First remove the plank from your own eye, and then you will see clearly to remove the speck from your brother's eye (Matthew 7:1-5).

God's message to us as wives is to take care of our own problems, wrong attitudes, and sins day by day...which brings us back to prayer. Pray for yourself, and pray for your husband.

*You redeem time when you...*fulfill your role as a wife. God created you to be a "helper" to your husband (Genesis 2:18). God's will for you is that you help your husband manage his minutes, his hours, his days, and his work. But are you thinking, *Wait a minute! What about me and my schedule and my minutes, hours, and days—and my work?* It doesn't seem fair, does it? But here is where trust comes in. You don't understand how God's plan works or how it will work out. Rather, you follow the advice of Proverbs 3:5-6:

> Trust in the LORD with all your heart,
>   and lean not on your own understanding;
> in all your ways acknowledge Him,
>   and He shall direct your path.

*You redeem time when you...*make the most of your time. Did you know the Bible has a lot to say about time management? One year as I read through my Bible, I marked every single passage that said anything about time and life management. In fact, at the end of that year I wrote a book titled *Life Management for Busy Women*[2] and drew principles from many of those passages. Remember, God isn't asking you to do anything apart from His strength and power. I love the verse "I can do all things through Christ who strengthens me" (Philippians 4:13).

*You redeem time when you...*pray for your husband to see his marriage as a team effort. God has asked you to "help" your husband. He hasn't asked you to "carry" him. There is obviously a fine line in some marriages where the husband isn't doing his share. For Eve to be a "helper" in the Garden of Eden meant Adam was busy doing work.

*You redeem time when you...*work in priority order. What do I mean by priority order? Again, looking at God's will, if you are a wife and you have children, then next to God, these are your priorities. Your day will be redeemed if these people are prayed for and cared for. Beyond that, everything else is secondary. You honor God and bless your family when they are your priority, as was the case with the Proverbs 31 wife and mother: "She watches over the ways of her household" (verse 27).

*You redeem time when you...*in addition to prayer, sit down with your husband and discuss how you can work as a team to accomplish all that God is asking of you in your marriage and with the family. What steps could you both take to gain better control of your time and your lives? One step you can take is to pray for your husband to want to manage his time well.

Time is important to God, and it was so important to Moses that he asked God to help him manage it. Because you are a busy woman who spends her days multitasking, you are very aware of time—and how little you have to spare! Maybe more than anything, you are praying that your husband would be understanding when you get a little frazzled. Most husbands I know are helpful with the kids and the kitchen. If you have one of those, praise and thank him!

Also, when it comes to your husband, do as Colossians 3:12 says and put on a heart of compassion and kindness. Keep in your mind and your heart the fact that most husbands in today's economy are under as much stress as you are, but in different ways. So pray to take this gentler, softer, more godly approach. Whether your husband is operating on a routine schedule and comes home to you and the family every evening, or he is in a tent in Afghanistan for 18 months, or he is submerged in the Pacific Ocean on a tour of duty, or he travels every week for his job, or he works rotating shifts at the plant, he needs your prayers.

Your role is to pray for your day and your time, and to pray for his day and his time. Prayer will help guard your heart from bitterness, loneliness, fear, disappointment, discouragement, anger, and self-pity. And as you pray for your husband's day—wherever he is and whatever it is he does for his job—you are investing in his life. Your prayers are an act of love, and you will find yourself involved in his work rather than resenting it. You will be *for* him, not *against* him. Again, you will be his number one cheerleader, supporter, and encourager.

I mentioned that Moses asked God to help him manage his time. Here's his prayer—another prayer for you to pray for yourself and your dear one!

A Prayer to Pray from the Heart of Moses
Psalm 90:12

Teach us to number our days,
that we may gain a heart of wisdom.

Chapter 10

Praying for Your Husband's Purity

You, O man of God, flee these things
and pursue righteousness, godliness,
faith, love, patience, gentleness.

1 TIMOTHY 6:11

*J*can never hear, read, or think about purity without remembering a course on friendship evangelism Jim and I attended as new Christians. We were so in love with Jesus and excited about knowing God that we wanted to learn how to share the good news of Jesus with others. A key part of our training included memorizing Bible verses to share. One of those verses was about God. I can still remember it today: "You are of purer eyes than to behold evil, and cannot look on wickedness" (Habakkuk 1:13).

I have to say, from that moment onward I had a better understanding of God and His 100-percent pure nature. Our call to grow in godliness means we are to strive for this kind of purity. We too are to refuse to look upon evil and any form of wickedness. That's a tall order in today's sensual society.

Like it or not, temptation is all around us, and no one, male or female, is immune. Not even Eve, who was created perfect and perfectly sinless by God and placed in a world without sin, was immune.

Accountability—Don't Leave Home Without It

Yet look at what Eve did in the Garden of Eden. Genesis chapter 3 opens with Eve alone in the garden with a stranger, a very *strange* stranger—a talking snake. Masterfully, this serpent tempted Eve to doubt God and His instructions and provision for her.

The age-old question is this: Where was Eve's husband, Adam? Maybe in your own mind you are shouting along with me, "Eve, no! D-O-N-'T DO IT! Go find your husband. Something is wrong—terribly wrong!" The Bible doesn't say anything about Adam at this point. Maybe he was off somewhere else in the garden admiring the beauty of his surroundings.

Whatever happened, the fact is Eve was alone and therefore without accountability. When temptation came, she had no one to give her a thumbs up or a frown and shake of the head. There was no one to support her or offer any words of advice or caution. She was left on her own to deal with the suggestions of the serpent—the devil (see Revelation 12:9).

And the result? Both Eve and her husband were judged and disciplined by God.

One reason I'm using Eve as an example is to point out that the lack of accountability, whether for you or your husband, can have disastrous results, as Genesis 3 graphically portrays.

Another example in which a lack of accountability got a man and woman into trouble appears in 2 Samuel 11. By this time King David had enjoyed years of immense success. This, in turn, may have weakened his acknowledgment and dependence upon God for wisdom, protection, and victory in battle.

Also, as king, David answered to no one. Like Eve, who "saw that the tree was good for food, that it was pleasant to the eyes" (Genesis 3:6), David's eyes also betrayed him. The Bible reports, "He saw a woman bathing and the woman was very beautiful to behold" (2 Samuel 11:2). After David noticed the woman from his rooftop, instead of continuing his walk or turning away, he chose to continue watching. Because David was a king, and because the woman's husband was gone from home, no one held either of them accountable and stopped them from making a series of really bad, life-altering decisions.

Purity Takes Two

As we think about David and Bathsheba, the woman who was bathing, we cannot point the finger of blame and say, "It was definitely David's fault!" or, "No, it was that woman's fault." That's because purity works both ways. It takes two agreeing or consenting people to commit adultery—or any other sin they agree on.

For instance, it's easy for couples to get caught up in the excitement of whatever is happening in the world and the people around them. For some, it's keeping up with the Joneses. These couples buy into the latest cars, houses, or exotic luxury vacations. It's not long before they are up to their necks in debt. What's even worse for Christian couples is when this kind of worldly behavior clouds their spiritual discernment and judgment to the point that the choices they make have grave implications on their spiritual growth and maturity. We certainly see this in the following portrait of a couple in the Bible who "agreed together" to sin (Acts 5:9).

Meet Ananias and Sapphira. In the early church, God was doing amazing things in the lives of the people. A spirit of love, unity, hospitality, and giving of goods and possessions prevailed in the hearts and minds of the early believers in the church at Jerusalem.

Many people from surrounding regions had received Christ as their Savior and become believers. With hearts filled to over-flowing with joy and compassion, these new Christians used up their money leaving their homes and occupations to travel to Jerusalem, wanting to be part of what was happening there at the center of Christianity. People like the man Barnabas, who had money or property, were selling their possessions and laying their offerings before the apostles to use as needed to help the people and the church (Acts 4:36-37).

Ananias and his wife, Sapphira, decided to follow the example of others and they too sold a piece of property. But this is where their story takes a tragic turn as together, in full agreement, they "kept back part of the proceeds" (Acts 5:2). The Bible does not give all the details. Had they promised God to give the whole amount, but later changed their minds and kept back part of the offering, while telling everyone it was the full amount? We don't know.

But we do know that the apostle Peter discerned their deception and described the ramifications of their sin. They had committed two offenses: First, they both had lied to God, the Holy Spirit, which was bad enough. And second, they lied publicly, which revealed their spiritual hypocrisy. This husband-and-wife team wanted others to see how "godly and wonderfully generous they were" because of the sacrificial nature of their gift, when, in fact, they kept a part of the offering for themselves.

You can read the full account of this sinful couple in Acts 5:1-11. I warn you now: It is an extremely sobering story that delivers a serious lesson to individuals about greed and lying, and to couples about agreeing to sin together.

God has given you your partner in marriage for, among other purposes, being a sounding board. The two of you should be a stronger, purer, greater force for doing what's right than either of you by yourselves would be. The two of you "have each other's back," and can hold each other accountable when something seems to be going in a wrong direction. As a couple, you should have a multiplying effect for good. You should bring out the best in each other, spurring you both in your growth as a couple after God's own heart.

The Bible's account relays that both Ananias and Sapphira were in agreement about their deception. Together, they had hatched up this clever little scheme. One or both of them had to know that what they were planning wasn't right. Surely one of them could have said something like, "No, I can't go along with this. This is wrong, and I don't want anything to do with it." Their story could have had a completely different ending—a good and honest ending.

Instead of being a dynamic for good, Ananias and Sapphira's deceit was such a strong threat to the infant church that God Himself took the ultimate action against them and killed them both.

In a marriage relationship, it is far too easy for us to bring out the worst in each other rather than the best. Don't let that be true of you as a wife. Commit yourself fully to doing as the Proverbs 31 woman did:

> The heart of her husband safely trusts her;
>   so he will have no lack of gain.
> She does him good and not evil
>   all the days of her life (Proverbs 31:11-12).

Praying for Purity

And so we pray! As we now address praying for purity for our husbands, I want you to latch on to this preliminary verse to pray for you and your man. We'll get to our key verse to pray for your husband in a minute. For now I want us to consider the teachings of Job 31:1 and Psalm 101:3. These verses contain commitments to purity that you can make for yourself and pray for your husband as well. Read the verses first. Then pray!

> I have made a covenant with my eyes; why then should I look upon a young woman? (Job 31:1).

> I will set nothing wicked before my eyes (Psalm 101:3).

My Prayer for Us as a Couple
Job 31:1 and Psalm 101:3

Holy God, I pray personally to make "a covenant with my eyes." I pray this also for my husband—that, with Your help and by Your grace, together we would avoid anything that could threaten our purity. I pray that _____ and I "will set nothing wicked before [our] eyes." Help us please, dear Lord!

Now, as we dive into the heart of this chapter on purity, I'm thinking you will agree with me on this point as we pray for our husbands. There are many titles given in the Bible for special men who served God and contributed mightily to the well-being of those around them. But the one title I want to be true and real for my husband is that he would be a "man of God." This title is found in 1 Timothy 6:11, and that's the kind of man I'm praying for my partner in life to be. You can pray the same for your husband. As you pray the prayer below, insert your husband's name in the blanks.

My Prayer for My Husband
1 Timothy 6:9,11

Gracious Father, I lift my husband before You and pray that _____ would be a man of God, that _____ would flee foolish and harmful lusts— those things that would tempt him to sin. I pray that instead, he would pursue righteousness, godliness, faith, love, patience, and gentleness.

The term *man of God* identifies such a man as God's personal possession. This title was given to Timothy, one of the apostle Paul's most trusted disciples. Paul had been working with Timothy for 15 years by the time the letter of 1 Timothy was written. The fact Paul gave this title to Timothy makes it clear that Paul held him in high regard for his spiritual strength, maturity, and purity. But that didn't keep Paul from wanting to give Timothy further instruction.

This should be your mind-set as well. You might have the greatest, most mature Christian husband on the planet. If so, praise God to the heavens—and keep on praying. Don't let his present walk with the Lord and victories over sin and against temptation keep you from continuing to pray for his purity. In fact, the more godly your husband is, the greater the need is for you to be praying for him. Satan would love nothing better than to topple a "man of God."

Other men in the Bible are also called a "man of God." As a man of God, your husband would be in the company of men like...

Moses—The phrase "man of God" first appears in Deuteronomy 33:1 to describe Moses, the great deliverer of God's people.

Samuel—The first of the prophets and also a judge in Israel, Samuel was given this title "man of God" in 1 Samuel 9:6.

Elijah and Elisha—These two were among the greatest prophets in the Old Testament, and were called men of God (1 Kings 17:18 and 2 Kings 4:7).

David—God used the title "a man after My own heart" to refer to David in Acts 13:22. Even with all his faults, David was referred to as "the man of God" in Nehemiah 12:24.

All of these Old Testament uses of "man of God" point to individual men who represented God by proclaiming His Word and upholding His truths even in the face of opposition or persecution. When you pray for your husband to be this kind of man, you are asking God to strengthen and fortify him to stand in the tradition of godly Old and New Testament men. Go ahead and ask this for your man! Ask it fervently and constantly every single day.

As you pray for your husband to be a man of God, keep these two requests at the top of your list:

Pray about the things your husband should avoid and flee from. Begin by praying for your husband to flee from harmful and sinful situations. You are praying for him to flee from things like false teaching, greed, a love of money, and foolish and harmful lusts (see 1 Timothy 6:3-10). Paul wanted Timothy's character to stand in sharp contrast with that of the false teachers. False teachers were greedy and worldly. God's man, however, is to be righteous and heavenly minded.

Like Timothy, your husband needs to realize there are certain things he absolutely must avoid at all costs. As the saying goes, he is not to see how close he can get to the edge of sinning without falling. No, he is to see how far away he can get from sin. God's man is to flee—to run in the opposite direction!—from sexual sin and idolatry (1 Corinthians 6:18 and 10:14).

If you are looking to fine-tune your prayers, here are a few more requests you can ask of the Father. Your goal is to pray that your life-mate will determine that anything that could replace God's rightful and high and exalted place in his heart is out. The list of these "idols of the heart" includes the love of money, selfish pride, the desire for worldly possessions, and even hobbies. Such a prayer list encompasses anything that would deflect your husband's focus on loving and obeying God and His commands found in the Bible.

Pray for the things your husband should seek and follow after. As fast as your husband is to flee and *run away from* those things that would corrupt him, he is to *run full-out toward* spiritual purity. Fleeing sin is half the battle, but he must equally continue to actively pursue holy living.

Think of it this way: It's like your husband is in a race toward the goal of holiness. If he stops, that which is behind him—sin—will catch him and he will miss the goal. And just to be clear, Paul lists six virtues in 2 Timothy 2:22 that every man, including your husband and mine, must pursue to merit the privileged title "man of God." Here we go, dear wife—this is your prayer list for your husband!

Righteousness—This has to do with external or outward behavior. This means your husband does what is right in his dealings with people and in his relationship with God. As God's man, he is known for doing what is right because his lifestyle is a reflection of his obedience to God's commands. Pray that your husband does not settle for a life of compromise.

Godliness—Just as righteousness concerns outward behavior, godliness is all about your husband's heart and his attitudes and motives. Jesus said, "Out of the abundance of the heart his mouth speaks" (Luke 6:45). Right behavior flows from a right heart, which means right motives. Proverbs 4:23 has this advice: "Keep your heart with all diligence, for out of it spring the issues of life."

Faith—This means trusting in God for everything. God's man has complete confidence in God's might, mandate, plan, provision, promises, and purposes. Pray for your husband, your man of God, to trust God to keep and fulfill His Word. This trust will motivate your husband to fulfill whatever the Bible asks of him as a provider, husband, and father.

Love—God's kind of love is unconditional love. This kind of love is bottomless, unrestrained, and embraces love for God, his family, other believers, and the lost. God's man understands the significance of His Lord's instructions in Matthew 22:37-39—love God and love your neighbor.

Patience—This can also be translated "perseverance" (NASB). This refers to being able to endure and bear up under difficult circumstances, even for a very long time, without losing your temper and becoming impatient, agitated, angry, or vengeful. What a great quality to be praying for in your husband—and yourself. For him to possess this quality will bless you as his wife, and his children. How marvelous! And, of course, patience in you will do the same and bless your spouse and children.

Gentleness—This means kindness or meekness. In the original Greek text of the New Testament, this is the only place this term appears. What wife wouldn't want this quality in her husband? Even though you are praying for your man to be strong, decisive, godly, wise, and a leader, you are also praying that his life and roles are marked by Christlike humility. He follows his Savior's appeal to "take My yoke upon you and learn from Me, for I am gentle and lowly in heart" (Matthew 11:29).

Beyond Prayer, What Can You Do?

Understand how temptation works. We watched in horror what happened to Eve in the Garden of Eden and to King David on his rooftop. In both cases, the eyes were involved in the temptation and the sin that resulted.

> When the woman saw that the tree was good for food, that it was pleasant to the eyes...she took of its fruit and ate (Genesis 3:6).

> David...saw a woman bathing, and the woman

was very beautiful to behold. So David sent and inquired about the woman...sent messengers, and took her...and he lay with her (2 Samuel 11:2-4).

First, be sure you understand that temptation is not the same as sin. Jesus was tempted for 40 days in the wilderness, but He never sinned. He never succumbed or gave in to the temptations. We, however, will sometimes give in to sin before we are even tempted all of 40 seconds!

Read 1 John 2:16 below to learn how the process of temptation lures us—and our husbands—into sinning.

> For all that is in the world—
> the lust of the flesh,
> the lust of the eyes, and
> the pride of life—
> is not of the Father but is of the world
> (1 John 2:16).

As you can see, temptation comes from three sources:

— from lust of the flesh and its inherent nature to be involved in evil things. This was David's problem.

— from the lust of the eyes, which deceives us by making what is evil look good. This was Eve's problem.

— from a pride that produces haughtiness or an overly inflated opinion of yourself. This was Ananias and Sapphira's problem.

Both you and your husband are bombarded by these kinds of temptations many times each day. So your prayers for purity should include sexual purity, but have a much broader scope than just sexual purity.

Understand men and women are different, especially regarding sex. I know sex is only one area of temptation, but infidelity is on the "top five" of most lists of reasons for divorce created by both lawyers and counselors. So obviously, sex with each other is important! I know this is nothing new, but wives with their busy schedules of juggling jobs, kids, and the home sometimes forget they are ignoring their husbands' sexual needs.

The apostle Paul was also concerned that couples were withholding their bodies from each other. He hinted at what might happen if this was not corrected. He counseled, "Do not deprive one another except with consent for a time, that you may give yourselves to fasting and prayer; and come together again so that Satan does not tempt you because of your lack of self-control" (1 Corinthians 7:5). Make sure your husband has no reason to be looking at or thinking about other women. What Jesus said applies to you and your husband and his struggle to stay pure: "The spirit indeed is willing, but the flesh is weak" (Matthew 26:41).

Communicate openly about the kinds of temptations you both are facing. In the verse we are praying for our husbands in this chapter, the context was greed and worldly behavior. This sounds familiar, doesn't it? It was a problem for Ananias and Sapphira, and it's sure true for our world today.

As a wife, evaluate whether you are contributing to any problems your husband is having with temptation in any areas. If there is a problem, ask yourself and your husband what you can do to help. Analyze if an extravagant lifestyle or excessive spending on your part is forcing your husband to devise ways to make extra money. This can cause him to work more and be at home less, increasing other kinds of temptation. If he feels the need to make more money, he may actually consider some opportunities that might not be considered illegal, but could be shady or risky. Maybe you need to put the brakes on spending. Maybe as a couple you need to get some financial counseling, to find someone to help the two of you dig yourselves out of a financial mess that's forcing your family to compromise its Christian principles.

There's also a need to keep the lines of communication open when it comes to sexual issues and especially the frequency each of you desires sex. If there are issues, again, together seek counsel. As with all the issues you and your husband are facing and will face, if you can talk about it, you can resolve it. As I often say, "A problem defined is half solved!"

My husband Jim and I were counseled early in our Christian marriage to schedule regular getaways. As we joyfully discovered, this is one of the best ways to keep the fires of passion burning in both of you. Find a babysitter or arrange with friends to exchange babysitting responsibilities for even one night. Just a single night away from the house, the children, and the myriad of responsibilities that come with a home and family allows the two of your to refocus on each other and your marriage.

Make up quickly. Marriage is a relationship between you, your husband, and God. It's like the three sides of a triangle. If you and your husband are angry with each other, it affects both of your relationships with God. In 1 Peter 3:7, husbands are advised to be sensitive to their wife's needs or suffer the consequence that their prayers will not be answered.

The principle of that verse works both ways. "Do not go to bed angry" is good advice for any married couple. Or, if you want it in stronger language, the Bible says, "Do not let the sun go down on your wrath" (Ephesians 4:26). Be quick to initiate the reconciliation and begin to once again reap God's blessings of a happy heart, a happy home, a really happy husband, and happy kids! Ahhhh, how sweet that will be—heaven on earth!

A Prayer to Pray from the Heart of David
Psalm 51:10 (NIV)

Create in me a pure heart, O God,
and renew a steadfast spirit within me.

Chapter 11

Praying for Your Husband's Speech

Let no corrupt word proceed out of your mouth,
but what is good for necessary edification,
that it may impart grace to the hearers.

EPHESIANS 4:29

Oh, those junior high pastors! They are most certainly a unique breed. They are forever thinking up creative ways to get their biblical points across to a restless audience. At least that was the case with the junior high pastor who taught our teenage daughters. My Jim and I still thank God that our girls had a good one. No, make that a great one!

Even before our girls could pile into the backseat of the car to head for their Bible study, they were already talking about the evening's Bible lesson. There was never any way to guess what Pastor Eric would come up with!

Well, our family (now including eight teen and preteen grandchildren who have heard this tale of the tongue repeated at family get-togethers) still talks about one memorable evening—and one memorable truth from the Bible. The youth pastor was teaching through the book of James and had arrived at James 3:5-8, a passage about the tongue. Earlier that day, Pastor Eric had gone to the grocery store and purchased a two-pound cow tongue. Then that evening, while he taught about how ugly the human tongue can be and the damage that unguarded speech can do, he passed the cow tongue around so each teen could look at it, smell it, and touch it. I don't have to tell you what an indelible impression this visual aid made on our girls and all their friends! They have never forgotten that particular lesson...and neither have we.

What James wrote about the human tongue, of course, is correct—it can be ugly. It is described in the Bible as "a fire, a world of iniquity...[which] defiles the whole body, and sets on fire the course of nature...no man can tame the tongue" (James 3:5-8).

As you pray for your husband in this area of his life, realize you are actually praying for two things. First, you will be praying for what we generally call communication, which especially applies to his interactions with you as his wife and with any children you have, as well as with the people he talks with at work.

The other aspect of speech is the actual words that come out of your husband's mouth—that is, the words and speech patterns that indicate what's in your husband's heart.

Speech Exposes the Heart

In the Bible the heart is seen as the seat of human emotion. You cannot hide what is in your heart because, sooner or later, your speech will reveal exactly what is within you. The Pharisees, the legalists of Jesus' day, believed they could be "religious" by following a set of external rules. For example, they meticulously watched what they ate and drank and how much money they gave at the temple. Jesus exposed their religion by rules. Note what He said:

> Those things which proceed out of the mouth come from the heart, and they defile a man. For out of the heart proceed evil thoughts, murders, adulteries, fornications, thefts, false witness, blasphemies. These are the things which defile a man, but to eat with unwashed hands does not defile a man (Matthew 15:18-20).

Praying for Your Husband's Heart Condition

Just about every wife I know and have talked with (and including myself!) worries about their husband's heart at one time or another. We wonder if everything is okay. We fret about our guy's food choices and lack of exercise and the stress he faces on the job. Unfortunately we even succumb to nagging, pleading, begging, lecturing, and we even strip the house of any and all "bad" foods. What we should be doing is praying and, of course, providing healthy meals.

Worry, no matter what the object, is our signal to pray, which means most wives pray for their husband's heart! You might even be like me and have a husband with a physical heart condition that is a concern for daily prayer. The physical heart is critical to the health and physical well-being of our husbands.

But what is even more critical is our husband's *spiritual* heart condition. As we learned from the above words of Jesus, everything flows from the heart. The heart is what determines behavior. The basic issue of behavior, including a person's speech, will always be determined by what's going on in that person's heart.

That's why God cautions us, "Keep your heart with all diligence, for out of it spring the issues of life" (Proverbs 4:23).

I'm sure you and I agree that we certainly have plenty to worry about in our own speech and behavior. I've had days—usually the "day after" some giant behavioral failure on my part—when I pray before I even get out of bed, "Today, Lord, I'm not going to...lose it...blow up...yell at the children...be harsh with my husband." I see (or rather, "hear") a problem, acknowledge the problem, pray for God's help with the problem, and make a plan to eliminate or fix the problem. As a young mom, my plan many days was "I *will not* scream at the children today. I *will not* scream at the children today. I will *not scream* at the children today..."

Yes, we ladies have our own speech issues. And the same is true of our husbands. We are usually worried about their external behavior, about what is seen and heard. That's because it affects us and our children, and contributes to how others view us and what they think of our husbands. We tend to worry more about the *what* of his speech rather than the *why*. When we do this—when we focus on the volume, vocabulary, and tone of voice with which it was said—we miss the root cause of our husband's behavior. We miss his heart condition. As Jesus stated,

> A good man out of the good treasure of his heart brings forth good; and an evil man out of the evil treasure of his heart brings forth evil. For out of the abundance of the heart his mouth speaks (Luke 6:45).

And so we pray. Sure, we pray for our man's behavior and his speech. But taking our cue from Jesus, first we pray specifically for his heart.

Pray for a new heart—God promised Israel in the Old Testament—and by extension, all believers today—that He would change their hearts with salvation. He promised, "I will put a new spirit within them, and take the stony heart out of their flesh, and give them a heart of flesh" (Ezekiel 11:19).

Maybe your husband's behavior is the result of a "stony heart." His heart has never been transformed. He may say and think he is a believer in Christ. But if his is not "a heart of flesh"—a heart that has been transformed by Christ—his actions will say something different. As Jesus explained, "Out of the heart proceed evil thoughts, murders, adulteries, fornications, thefts, false witness, blasphemies" (Matthew 15:19).

If you see your husband's lifestyle in the verse above—in Matthew 15:19—and he is not a Christian, your first emergency response is to pray, pray, and pray some more every single day. Pray for God to save him, to open his heart to the Person of Christ, to make him a new creature in Christ, to create in him a clean heart.[1] Plead with God to take "the stony heart" out of your husband and to give him "a heart of flesh." This is to be the essence of your prayers.

Think of praying for your husband's heart as a part of your prayer workout every single day. Your first and ongoing prayer needs to be asking God to change his heart. That's because any change that *you* are hoping for in your husband's manner and values and lifestyle will be merely superficial. That's not enough. Your basic prayer must be for his salvation, for him to have a new heart, which only God can accomplish.

But what about a husband who is a Christian, yet is slipping deeper into worldly behavior and attitudes and speech? You pray!

Pray for a straying heart—If your husband is a believer and is exhibiting errant behavior and straying from God's standards, it is an indication that he has a "straying heart." His actions are indicating that he has taken his eyes off God and His Son and is drifting farther and farther away from God's desires for his life.

How can you help?

Pray for the Holy Spirit to convict your husband of his straying heart. Sometimes a man can get so obsessed with his job or other things like hobbies, entertainment, or food that he takes his focus off of his relationship with God. Instead of walking by the Spirit, he starts walking in a fleshly way. He may even fall back into some old habits from his non-Christian past.

And don't forget to pray about what God wants you to do. Maybe if and when you believe the time is right and your heart is right, you can lovingly talk with your husband with grace in your heart (Colossians 3:16) as a fellow believer and as his wife and as "co-heirs with Christ" (Romans 8:17).

Unfortunately, many wives make their first move in total frustration. They strike out in anger. They rip into their husband in a full-out attack. It always helps me to remember: "Two wrongs never make a right." When your husband is misbehaving, that is Wrong #1. But if you scream, yell, have a fit, blow up, or lash out in anger, that is Wrong #2. When a wife behaves in this way, she is as wrong as her husband is.

Please, don't let this be you! Look to God. He will give you all of the words, wisdom, and gentleness—and self-control!—you need to "impart grace to the hearers" (Ephesians 4:29).

Two Ways to Improve Communication

Every couple has to work at communication skills. In fact, according to online sources, communication appears consistently on the top-ten lists of reasons couples divorce. One of my favorite books on this all-important subject has a title that says it all: *Communication: Key to Your Marriage.* And the subtitle is just as true: *The Secret to True Happiness.*[2]

I'm sure you have had times when you've had issues with your husband's choice of words or his means of communication. And guess what? I'm just as sure there have been times when he has struggled with your methods of communicating with him.

Whatever your problem is with your husband's speech, one way to improve communication is to pray. Pray for your husband to understand how important speech and communication are in your marriage and in his parenting. This is the easy path. All you do is pray, and God does the rest!

The second way to improve communication in your marriage is much harder: You must deal with yourself. Evaluate how much you may be contributing to the downward communications and speech spiral between you and your husband. Can you put your finger on what you may be doing that affects your husband negatively?

The next time you go head-to-head verbally, before you lash out at your husband like a cat with her claws out, and before you jump in to vent at your husband about his speech, and before you lecture him, and before you spout out Bible verses, stop!

Then immediately start praying. "Lord, what is the right thing to do here? Lord, help me. Give me wisdom."

This kind of response puts the brakes on an escalating argument. It gives you time to come up with a better plan for communicating your message and your heart to your husband—and with the words and demeanor that will make it easier for your husband to listen to you.

I'm sure you agree that this path of dealing with yourself is the harder path for sure. But think about it. You can't do anything about your husband's communication but pray for him, and pray about how the two of you can talk about what's happening in your marriage. But you can do *everything* about your own speech! Your choice of words can be soothing or sour, encouraging or exasperating. Unfortunately, it is all too easy for us to speak words that result in hurtful rather than helpful communication.

"A Continual Dripping"

Can you believe God uses the imagery of a constant drip to remind us of the need to improve our speech? It's true! Proverbs 19:13 says, "The contentions of a wife are a continual dripping." Ouch!

But it's true, and I've done it myself! This is what happens when you and I do things, including communicating, our way instead of God's way. We fail to pay attention to God's wise guidelines for our speech. And Proverbs has more to say about the negative side of communication. As you read the following passages, notice how the woman is described:

> Better to dwell in a corner of a housetop, than in a house shared with a contentious woman (Proverbs 21:9).
>
> Better to dwell in the wilderness, than with a contentious and angry woman (Proverbs 21:19).
>
> A continual dripping on a very rainy day and a contentious woman are alike (Proverbs 27:15).

I think you can see that the message is pretty clear. It's important to take care of your own speech before you obsess over your husband's speech. Analyze and pray about the way you communicate. It's far easier to say or think, "Well, my husband has changed. He's not the same man I married." But take a look at yourself in the mirror. Were you at one time in your marriage a happy, carefree, loving, considerate, and sweet wife?

It's easy to allow the years and the cares of life and the challenges of marriage to turn you into a crabby, cranky, nagging, quarrelsome, complaining, ill-tempered wife who is annoyed by just about everything her husbands does. And before you know it, *you* are like the constant drippings of a faucet.

You know how a dripping faucet can drive you crazy, don't you? Well, these proverbs report the same reaction taking place in husbands who have a "dripping faucet" for a wife. It can drive the husband crazy, and sadly, it can drive him away.

These verses that describe the "contentious woman" might seem like overkill, but I'm sure you get their message. Is some measure of this happening in your relationship with your husband? If so, you will want to make some dramatic changes right away. Your goal—and your remedy—is found in Proverbs 31:26: God's excellent woman "opens her mouth with wisdom, and on her tongue is the law of kindness."

A Word Rightly Spoken

Before we look at a verse you can pray for your husband's speech, here's a verse you might want to think and pray about yourself:

> Like apples of gold in settings of silver
> is a word spoken in right circumstances
> (Proverbs 25:11 NASB).

Dear wife, the kind of speech that God is asking of you is like gold apples set against a silver basket or sculpture or carving, or like gold earrings or other ornaments. Your speech, especially toward your husband, needs to have this same kind of beauty. Proverbs gives us this picture, and Proverbs also gives us a lot of guidance about how our communication can be godly and given in the right way at the right time. Your words are to be...

...soft. "A soft answer turns away wrath, but a harsh word stirs up anger" (Proverbs 15:1). The words you choose to use have an effect on your husband. Harsh, loud, caustic speech can lead to arguments and quarrels, while soft, gentle words bring about peace. And here's an astonishing fact: "A soft tongue can break hard bones" (Proverbs 25:15 TLB)!

...sweet. "Sweetness of the lips increases learning" or influence (Proverbs 16:21). Or, as this proverb reads in two other translations: "pleasant words are persuasive" (NLT); "gracious words promote instruction" (NIV).

...suitable. "Pleasant words are like a honeycomb, sweetness to the soul and health to the bones" (Proverbs 16:24). Kind words uttered in the right way at the right time have an almost medicinal effect on both the body and soul.

...scant. "In the multitude of words sin is not lacking, but he who restrains his lips is wise" (Proverbs 10:19). The more you talk, the more you are sure to slip up and sin! Another Bible translation is very vivid and down-to-earth in its language: "Too much talk leads to sin. Be sensible and keep your mouth shut" (NLT). Sometimes—no, *most* times—according to this verse, it is better to say nothing!

There can be no argument if only one of you is speaking.

...slow. "Be swift to hear, slow to speak, slow to wrath" (James 1:19). Make it your aim to "listen much, speak little, and not become angry" (TLB). Why? Because "the wrath of man does not produce the righteousness of God" (verse 20 NKJV).

Do you want your speech to be "apples of gold in settings of silver"? Then concentrate on speaking with godly wisdom when you communicate with your husband. Choose words that are soft, sweet, suitable, and, by all means, scant!

Your speech is your first priority. And it's something you can definitely do because it's completely up to you. And God is 100 percent willing to help you communicate His way—with love, with wisdom, and with sweetness. As you make strides in the speech department, you can also pray for your husband. Here's a prayer just for him. It's based on the verse that appears on the first page of this chapter. Better yet, you can read it in your Bible.

My Prayer for My Husband
Ephesians 4:29

Lord, help _____ choose his words carefully whenever he speaks at home or away. May what he says be good and helpful, an encouragement and a blessing to those who hear him. May the words of _____'s mouth please You.

Unpacking the Verse—What Does It Mean?

In Ephesians 4, Paul addressed the topic of how a transformed Christian should act—a believer's speech should be transformed by Christ, just like everything else in his life. After Paul told believers what they were not to say, he then told them what they should say. As you continue reading, open your heart to what Paul is teaching. Remember that these are God's instructions to all believers—male and female, single and married, husband...and wife.

What should not characterize your husband's speech—"Let no corrupt word proceed out of your mouth." As I looked into the meaning of "corrupt" I came across synonyms like *depraved, foul,* and *impure.* Another Bible translates "corrupt" as "unwholesome" (NASB).

And so you pray! Pray for your husband to not use foul language. This is totally out of character for a Christian. Off-color jokes, profanity, dirty stories, vulgarity, suggestive talk, and every other form of corrupt speech should be banished from his lips. Pray for God to keep his heart and mind—and mouth—pure.

Obviously this was an issue with the Christians at Ephesus, or Paul would not have needed to address this subject. And unfortunately, this problem hasn't changed. Today it is impossible to go out shopping or to a restaurant and not hear profanity and explicit language, many times coming even from children.

Most likely, your husband works in an environment where "unwholesome" language is the norm. So redouble your prayers each day for your husband. Pray that he will stand strong and remember the Bible's guidelines for his speech as set down in Ephesians 4:29:

Guideline #1: What not to say—
Let no corrupt word proceed out of your mouth,

Guideline #2: What to say—
but what is good for necessary edification,

Guideline #3: The purpose for all speech—
that it may impart grace to the hearers.

What should characterize your husband's speech—"...what is good for necessary edification, that it may impart grace to the hearers." Pray this lofty goal for all his speech—that it be edifying and encouraging, that it minister to and bless the hearer.

— Pray that your husband's words would be gracious, "like a honeycomb, sweetness to the soul and health to the bones" (Proverbs 16:24).

— Pray that you and your children are the first recipients of his gracious speech—that his words would "impart grace to the hearers," that what he says would be helpful, constructive, encouraging, and uplifting.

— Pray that his speech would be "gracious" and edify all those who cross his path each and every day.

— Pray for your husband's awareness of the need to watch his words. Pray that he will adhere to these instructions from Colossians 4:6: "Let your speech always be with grace, seasoned with salt, that you may know how you ought to answer each one."

— Pray that your husband will be a man of his word, that others can trust what he says—"Let your 'Yes' be 'Yes,' and your 'No,' 'No'" (James 5:12).

— Pray for your husband to speak out for what is right. That's what a godly man must do, according to Proverbs 31:8-9:

> Open your mouth for the speechless,
> in the cause of all who are appointed to die.
> Open your mouth, judge righteously,
> and plead the cause of the poor and needy.

— Pray for your husband's speech and conduct, that he would be a man of "good behavior...not violent...gentle, not quarrelsome...hav[ing] a good testimony among those who are outside" (1 Timothy 3:1-7).

— Pray that your husband's speech will draw men to the Savior. Every Christian is an ambassador for Christ. Your husband's speech and conduct may be the only Bible many people ever read: "We are ambassadors for Christ, as though God were pleading through us" (2 Corinthians 5:20).

— Pray for God to be pleased with your husband's words. Pray that, like King David, this would be the desire of your husband's heart: "Let the words of my mouth and the meditation of my heart be acceptable in Your sight, O Lord" (Psalm 19:14).

When your husband's speech pleases God, he will be honoring God and his family, blessing the church body, and giving the world a chance to be in the presence of a man of God.

Words

A careless word may kindle strife.
A cruel word may wreck a life.
A brutal word may smite and kill.
A gracious word may smooth the way.
A joyous word may light the day.
A timely word may lessen stress.[3]

A Prayer to Pray from the Heart of David
Psalm 141:3

Set a guard, O LORD, over my mouth;
keep watch over the door of my lips.

Chapter 12

Praying for Your Husband to Act with Courage

Be strong and of good courage; do not be
afraid, nor be dismayed, for the LORD
your God is with you wherever you go.

JOSHUA 1:9

*O*rdinary days." How many situations can arise in an ordinary day in your life that cause fear or doubt or a lack of confidence to well up in your stomach or maybe your throat? I've made my own short list from some of my days that began in the usual way. You know, quiet house, quiet world, perfect quiet time topped off with a magnificent sunrise, all of which occur before the world starts to rock and roll. Then somewhere along the way of the day something occurs that produces disturbing emotions:

- Witnessing a teen boy and his dad in a physical and verbal brawl
- Enduring a super-bumpy plane ride

- Having a flat tire on a dark stretch of road at night
- Facing a public performance or ministry or work responsibility
- Suffering through a medical procedure to determine the cause of a physical problem
- Helplessly watching a child or grandchild suffer a long-term medical condition
- Coping with a stressful relationship with a family member
- Taking your husband to the parade grounds on base before he deploys to a foreign country

Courage in the Midst of Fear

It's easy to stand by and do nothing when something happens, isn't it? You tell yourself, *Just don't get drawn in. Let someone else get involved and take care of this.* Unfortunately, usually nobody does! We've all heard distressing stories of people dying in a public area because no one would stop to help or volunteer or even dial 911 for emergency services.

In this chapter we will talk about praying for our husbands to be men of courage. But you and I also need courage for a multitude of situations that require us to act or take a stand or speak up, or make a tough decision and do the hard thing. I know I do. After all, I created the list of situations above!

As we move through this topic, remember that courage is not the absence of fear. *Courage is having the ability to act in the midst of fear.* There are many inspiring examples of courage among the women in the Bible, but the faithful and fearless band of women who followed Jesus has to be at the top of my courage list! We will get to your husband in a minute; first, let's spend some girl time looking at these ladies who have instructed and inspired women for centuries to stand up, be strong, and with God's help, do what must be done.

The women at the cross—There are some women in the Bible who I simply cannot point to enough or think of often enough because they were so courageous in their faithfulness to our Lord Jesus, no matter what and regardless of danger or misunderstanding. They are the women who huddled at the cross and who, in spite of the risks and the possibility of bodily harm and criticism from others, courageously did the right thing.

Can you imagine the scene on the day Jesus died? The sky grew dark even though it was still day. Earthquakes occurred, splitting rocks and opening long-sealed tombs, and many of the dead saints of old rose from their graves and were walking about.

It was such a scary sight and experience that even the hardened Roman soldiers "feared greatly" (Matthew 27:54). And all but one of Jesus' disciples fled this horrifying scene of pure chaos, leaving their faithful Friend, Teacher, Master, Savior, and Lord during His hour of suffering and death.

Yet in the midst of this fearful, dangerous, and disturbing setting of agony and crazed activity we see that "many women who followed Jesus from Galilee, ministering to Him, were there looking on from afar" (verse 55). These women were truly courageous at a time when all normalcy disappeared and life spun out of control, causing those present to fear for their lives.

"Why," you may be asking along with me, "were these women so brave in the midst of a horrendous and life-threatening situation while others cowered or fled in fear?"

The answer is love—love for Jesus. Their love for their Friend and Teacher was so great it fought off their fears. They lived out the truth that "there is no fear in love; but perfect love casts out

fear" (1 John 4:18). And their faith in God was so strong and
steady that they acted with courage. Perhaps they were boldly
reminding themselves to rely on the Lord, as the psalmist did
in Psalm 56:4:

> In God I have put my trust;
> I will not fear.
> What can flesh do to me?

Faith in God is always the antidote for fear. Your need for
courage to fight off and withstand the fears of death, suffering,
loss, tragedy, illness, and sorrow finds its strength in the Lord.
And, as Jesus taught and warned, "In Me you may have peace.
In the world you will have tribulation; but be of good cheer, I
have overcome the world" (John 16:33). So when—not if—your
trials arrive, whatever they may be and whatever their magni-
tude, look to Jesus. Let Him and His presence displace your
fears with His courage.

In general, our opportunities to exhibit courage don't involve
danger. But fear is always an element in the midst of suffering
and pain. That's why the example of these women bolsters our
courage. Their faithfulness and their courage, however shaky, is
an example for us in our trying situations and encounters. Their
faith and trust in God empowered them with the bravery they
needed to face danger as they identified themselves with their
Savior, who was despised and rejected and being put to death.

This rag-tag group of women from all walks of life was willing to stand up for Jesus, to identify with Him, and to serve
Him to the very end. Do you have this kind of commitment
to the Lord and the things He stands for and against? If your
resolve is weak or lacking, pray! Ask God to deepen your love

and resultant faith for Jesus, so that you too will have the courage to live for Jesus each and every day, come what may.

The man who defended the cross—Now fast-forward some 1500 years from the time of Jesus and these noble women to 1517. Here we meet a 34-year-old German priest named Martin Luther. I've heard my husband share Martin Luther's story scores of times in sermons and pastors' conferences and men's groups as an example of standing up for what you believe—of having courage. So I'm passing on Jim's message to you.

In his day, Martin Luther became outraged that people were being taught that freedom from God's punishment of sin could be purchased with money. People were offered these "indulgences," which were described in an edict from Pope Leo X. Luther confronted the peddling of these indulgences with 95 statements that he nailed on the door of All Saints' Church in Wittenberg, Germany. This now-famous list criticized the Pope and explained that the sale of these "get out of hell free passes" were religiously incorrect. Christ's death was the only thing that could keep a person out of hell, not the payment of money to the church!

Luther knew the serious nature of his official summons due to his criticism of the sale of the indulgences. Yet he still appeared as ordered on April 17, 1521, before the Diet of Worms, a general assembly of the Catholic Church in the small town of Worms in Germany. There, Luther was presented with a list of his writings. He was then asked two questions: Were the books his, and did he stand by their contents?

Luther requested time to think about his answers. He was given until the next day to offer his reply. After Luther was dismissed, he prayed and consulted with friends. When he was brought before his accusers on the next day, he quickly confirmed he was the author of the writings. Then in response to the second question—Did he stand by their contents?—he said this:

> Unless I am convinced by the testimony of the Scriptures or by clear reason (for I do not trust either in the pope or in councils alone, since it is well known that they have often erred and contradicted themselves), I am bound by the Scriptures I have quoted and my conscience is captive to the Word of God. I cannot and will not recant anything, since it is neither safe nor right to go against conscience. May God help me. Amen.[1]

Martin Luther is also quoted as saying during the same meeting: "Here I stand. I can do no other." But regardless of the full extent of his statement, the effects of these now well-known Ninety-Five Theses were huge. Luther's courage—his willingness to stand true to his beliefs—was the spark that ignited the great Protestant Reformation.

Praying for Courage

We can only imagine the number of prayers that the women at the cross and Martin Luther sent flying heavenward during their ordeals. And we can only guess at the intensity and fervency of those prayers! For sure, all Christians are not only to pray for courage in the midst of fiery trials and distress, but also to pray regularly for courage.

God has four words for you or your husband when you must face, endure, or are surprised by life's challenges:

Do not be afraid.

These words were spoken by God to Joshua, who became the leader of the children of Israel after Moses died. Suddenly Joshua was expected to lead a massive group of people—more than two million of them! It's no wonder God had to repeatedly encourage His new leader. He spent a considerable amount of time bolstering Joshua's courage and admonishing him about the dangers of fear (Joshua 1:1-9).

So if God went to such great lengths to encourage His "man" to be courageous, shouldn't you and I be doing the same for our "man," our husband? That's why Joshua 1:9 is such an important verse for you to be praying for your husband: "Be strong and of good courage; do not be afraid, nor be dismayed, for the LORD your God is with you wherever you go."

My Prayer for My Husband
Joshua 1:9

Lord Jesus, thank You that You are beside my precious _____ right now and at all times. Help _____ to sense Your powerful presence when he needs to be courageous and live boldly as a Christian. Encourage _____ to speak up when it's the right thing to do and stand up in difficult situations. Amen.

Fear is often seen as being reserved for those who are weak. But Joshua was in no way weak. He was a bona fide leader after God's own heart, a worthy study in leadership himself. You can read his story in the book of Joshua in the Bible. Once you begin reading about him, you will quickly discover Joshua had a bad case of "the fears."

Joshua's position as leader of God's people, the Israelites (Joshua 1:1), got off to an immediate start. One minute Joshua was the servant and follower of Moses...and the next minute God had put him in charge.

It appears that with this sudden call to leadership, Joshua was fairly fearful and anxious. But God never rebuked Joshua's fear. He only instructed, exhorted, and encouraged Joshua to be strong and overcome his fear by trusting in Him. Joshua's fears were justified because of...

> Joshua's predecessor, Moses. Joshua was expected to follow in the sandals of the bigger-than-life-leader—the same Moses who talked to God and miraculously led the people of Israel out of the nation of Egypt. Then there was...

> Joshua's army, if you could call it that! His men were a ragtag band with little or no military training or experience in battle. And finally, there was...

> Joshua's enemy, who inhabited the land. Joshua had seen them himself. They were giants—literally. They were savage tribes who refused to give up their land without a fierce fight (Numbers 13:32; 14:45).

God knew Joshua, and He knows you and your husband too. He also knows that you are strong in many ways but still tend to have your own fears and doubts. But no worries! God told Joshua—and He speaks to you and your husband as well—to "be strong and of good courage." Why? And how? Because "the Lord your God is with you wherever you go."

So whatever you and your husband are currently facing or will face in the future, you can both draw on three reasons why you can always act with courage. These three reasons tell you why you never need to let fear immobilize you—why you can be courageous in fighting the battles the two of you are facing now and will face in the future.

Reason #1: Courage grows from God's character—God said to Joshua, "Be strong and courageous" (Joshua 1:9). God was like a coach—the ultimate coach—on the sidelines, encouraging Joshua to, in essence, "lead these people to victory—give them the land! You can do it, Joshua!"

"Why, Lord?" we might wonder along with Joshua.

"Because I swore to their fathers to give them possession of the land," the Lord explained (see verse 6).

End of discussion! God promised it, and...it was as good as done.

Joshua had to go to battle. That was settled. But God's purpose, promise, and pep talk meant Joshua could go into battle with courage, knowing that God, who cannot lie, had promised victory. God was not going to allow Joshua to fail nor fail to fulfill God's promise to the people.

Understanding God's character gives your husband and you assurance of His ability to fulfill the promises He has presented in His Word. He has promised you victory too: "Thanks be to God who *always* leads us in triumph in Christ" (2 Corinthians 2:14). And, like Joshua, you must trust God to do what He has promised.

Your triumph in God is a given. Your promised victory should give you courage and confidence in the battles you face and fight in everyday life. The confidence in God's promise of courage is what you are asking in prayer for your husband—a courage that comes from remembering and acknowledging the character of God. The saying is true: "You behave how you believe." If your husband believes in an all-powerful and a promise-keeping God, then he will have the courage to act on those beliefs. *That's* what you, dear wife, are praying for!

Reason #2: Courage multiplies with the knowledge of God's presence—"...for the LORD your God is with you." Log this well: God promised to be with Joshua. This is the third time God told His man, "Be strong and of good courage." And then the Lord added, "Do not be afraid, nor be dismayed." Why? "For the Lord your God is with you" (Joshua 1:9).

I'm sure your husband faces plenty of difficult situations, or maybe he is currently enduring an illness or injury. Or maybe he's preparing to attend a tough meeting at work or is involved in completing a rigorous, demanding commitment and he needs to hang in there and be brave. Or maybe he's giving a speech or teaching a lesson at church or a Bible study. All of these are situations where courage is needed. And so you pray!

I'm sure you can relate to some of these stressful situations as well. Everyone's been in a place where they needed to be brave and do well or make it through to the end. We all must at times be courageous. And so we pray!

I'm also sure you know how encouraging it is when you are nearby to cheer your husband on. Your support—and the knowledge you are praying—can provide the stimulus for him to do his best. Your very presence gives him extra courage to do the right thing.

Well, it's even more motivating for your husband to know that God is always nearby—right there with him, whether you are or not—no matter what happens and no matter where he goes. This was the secret to Joshua's courage. And it should be the secret to your husband's courage too as he makes his way through each and every challenge. Are you grasping how important it is to be praying for your husband to understand that God is with him?

Here's another thought about God's presence: One secret to having courage is realizing that fear is natural, but the presence of God right beside you, all the time, is supernatural. When you recall this truth, you have successfully begun to fight your fears and gain the strength and courage needed for the tasks—and challenges—the Lord brings your way. Strength is yours whenever you remember Jesus promised, "I am with you always, even to the end of the age" (Matthew 28:20), and "I will never leave you nor forsake you" (Hebrews 13:5).

Reason #3: Courage expands with God's guidance—"your God is with you wherever you go." Maybe Joshua was still wavering and wondering. Maybe he wasn't quite sure he wanted the job or could handle it. I'm sure your husband can relate! But whatever was going through Joshua's mind, God told him again, for the second time, "Be strong and very courageous" (Joshua 1:7). In essence, God coached his tentative handpicked man, "Take *even more* courage, Joshua!"

Why, Lord?

Because I am with you wherever you go!

God was saying, "Joshua, I will guide you by My very presence. I will be your battle plan and I will guide you to success! And I am giving you all the strength you will need to pull it off, to make it happen—to be successful."

God gave His man Joshua guidance, and He can give guidance to your man too. How? Today, God guides through His Word. So, as God cautioned Joshua, "Do according to all the law which Moses My servant commanded you" (verse 7). This is why you are praying for your husband to spend time reading the Bible, so he can do according to what he reads in it.

My husband Jim once told me about a championship football

team that was defeated by a weaker team. It didn't matter what play was run—the opponent seemed to know exactly how to defend against the play. The coaches on the stronger team were baffled as they tried to make sense of their loss. Then, sometime later, the mystery was solved: The opposing team had somehow obtained one of their team's playbooks. The stolen playbook gave the opposing team a guide to victory. They knew every play the other team might possibly attempt.

God knows all of Satan's plays, his entire bag of "tricks." And God has given your husband a playbook as well—the Bible. Whatever Satan may throw at your husband, however he may tempt your guy, the Bible has a defense. Being armed with the knowledge from God's playbook means your husband can make a strong, successful defense against fear and the flaming missiles of the evil one (Ephesians 6:16).

My praying friend and fellow devoted wife, purpose to pray for your husband to follow God's advice to Joshua. Pray he doesn't get distracted, take his eyes off of Jesus, and lose courage. That's what Peter did as he was miraculously walking on the water toward Jesus—he focused on the waves rather than on Christ and began to sink (see Matthew 14:29-30). Pray that your husband does not turn to the right or to the left, but stays focused on God and His playbook for his life. Then he will have good success...wherever he goes (see Joshua 1:8-9).

A Profile of Courage

In his 1955 Pulitzer Prize-winning book *Profiles in Courage*, the late president John F. Kennedy chronicled the life stories of eight US senators. He described and outlined how these men endured the pressures of public office—the risks to their careers, popularity with the people, defamation of their character—all with great courage.[2]

I understand that the word and act of *profiling* is not politically correct, and that profiling can be abused and cause great harm. The dictionary defines profiling as simply developing a list of characteristics that represent someone or something. So it is what we do with such a list that causes problems for some people. But if we develop a list of characteristics for, in our case, the quality of courage, what does courage look like so we know how to pray for its presence in our husbands?

Courage starts in the heart—Courage is not an instantaneous emotion or automatic response. The starting point for your husband's courage is his heart. Courage has a heartfelt cause. Joshua's cause was the conquest of the Promised Land. You are praying for your husband to develop a heart for God. If he believes strongly in something, like his faith, that faith will fan the flame of his courage. "As he thinks in his heart, so is he" (Proverbs 23:7).

Courage takes risks—Taking risks seems to be the common denominator of courageous people. I'm not talking about foolish, daredevil kinds of risks. I'm talking about risks of faith and conviction! The women who remained with Jesus at the cross took risks. So did Abraham when he left his home to travel to a strange land just because God told him to.

Missionaries also take risks. Our friends Tim and Nancy were literally "helicoptered out" of Liberia with only the clothes on their backs. They were allowed to take one thing only—and they each took one of their two children on their backs. What did they do after such an ordeal? Go home to safety? Write a letter of resignation to their mission organization? Take a long furlough? No, they courageously took the risk and went to another mission field and started over. Courage is not timid. Pray that your husband will boldly take risks to do whatever is right!

Courage attempts the impossible—It doesn't take much courage to do the ordinary. Doing the routine is simply doing your duty. But attempting the impossible takes audacity—or chutzpah. For example, what Nehemiah was considering was impossible. After all, for at least 90 years, many others had failed to rebuild the walls around Jerusalem and reestablish the city of God. Yet under Nehemiah's courageous, faith-filled leadership, the wall was rebuilt—in only 52 days! The next time your husband needs a dose of courage, remind him of how God helped Nehemiah. Doing what is right and what is God's will is always possible—with courage.

Courage takes a stand—Together, you and your husband spend your whole married life building your reputations and social position. Your reputations are important, as well they should be! But would you be willing to lose all that you've worked for if it meant standing up and showing your loyalty to Jesus Christ?

Today, many people treat the Bible and Jesus with contempt. Now is the time to step forward and give testimony to what Christ has done for you, individually and as a couple. Now is the time to be courageous and stand and be counted as followers of Jesus Christ. Hopefully others will stand alongside the two of you. But even if you must stand alone, you are not alone. Jesus Himself is with you!

Courage does the right thing—Courage never goes out of date. That's because it is always the right time to make the right choices. And it's no surprise that right choices are usually difficult choices. Courage does the right thing, which is the biblical thing. And courage does it even at the risk of being criticized or labeled as "politically incorrect." A strong prayer life, even if you are the only one praying, will guide you as you and your husband seek to do the right thing.

God Is Looking for Men and Women of Courage

God is looking for men and women to fight moral, physical, political, and spiritual battles. He is looking for those who possess the spiritual courage to trust Him and take their faith in Him into the battles of daily life. He is looking for individuals and couples who possess the courage to

> stand up for Christ in public, at work, and at home;
>
> model godly character to others;
>
> guide your family out of worldliness and into godliness; and
>
> live a consistent life for Christ, regardless of the cost.

Can God count on you? I know you can't answer for your husband, but you can answer for yourself and pray that if not today, someday soon your husband will join you in God's circle of courage. It's okay if you don't feel very courageous, and your husband is not quite there either. There is no shame in that. All the giants of the faith, like Abraham, Joshua, and Nehemiah, had times when they faltered, but they did not fall. Enjoy and share with your husband these few steps that will strengthen your courage as a couple.

1. You can always draw strength, power, and resolve from God's character, God's Word, and God's presence (Joshua 1:8-9).

2. You should determine your standards. Know what you believe, and why. Courage emerges once you are willing to fight for those standards.

3. Your courage needs to be tested. Don't be afraid to stretch yourself. Courage comes as you consistently overcome hurdles, which makes you stronger for the next test of courage.

4. You will find yourself encouraged when you remember that God is with you. He's there—always right there with you—to help you fight your battles whenever and wherever they are fought. Be strong and courageous! "If God is with us and we're with Him, we have nothing to fear."[3]

***

A Prayer to Pray from the Heart of Peter
1 Peter 5:10

May the God of all grace,
who called us to His eternal glory by Christ Jesus...
perfect, establish, strengthen, and settle you.

Chapter 13

Praying for Your Husband's Walk with God

*Walk in the Spirit, and you shall
not fulfill the lust of the flesh.*

GALATIANS 5:16

When you think of apples, what state comes to mind—
Washington State, right? You are correct! Jim and I
live in the state of Washington. And we have an apple tree right
in our front yard. That means each year we get to witness God's
process for the miraculous production of apples—from start to
finish. Talk to anyone who has a healthy, productive fruit tree,
and you will hear about all the work that is required to care for,
improve, and increase a crop of fruit. The person who tends a
fruit tree nurtures, fertilizes, waters, prunes, trains, sprays, and
protects the tree. And a year-long effort is finally—*finally!*—
rewarded with abundant fruit for cooking, freezing, drying, and
even canning. The hard work has its payday.

As I think about our amazing apple tree, I can't help but wonder about the fruit of our lives as Christians. Should you and I pay any less attention to our own fruitfulness—in our case, the spiritual kind of fruit—than we do to an apple tree? Shouldn't we be actively cultivating the fruit of the Spirit in our lives so we reflect the glory of God and the beauty of Christ?

What exactly can we do to stimulate the growth of spiritual fruit? Are there any practical steps we can take to get our act together so we become more like Jesus? And another question that is just as important is this: What can we do to encourage our husbands to want to take these practical steps toward being fruit-bearing believers?

As we continue to consider scriptures we can pray for our husbands, we now come to Galatians 5:16: "Walk in the Spirit, and you shall not fulfill the lust of the flesh." Before we look at how we can pray this verse for our husbands, let's begin at the spiritual starting point.

The Gift of the Holy Spirit

If you and your husband have children, they possess part of your essence—your DNA. Similarly, when you accepted Jesus as your Lord and Savior, you become a new creation possessing a part of God's personality, a part of His DNA, so to speak. He passed on to you the Holy Spirit through your union with His Son, Jesus Christ. This gift from God is described as "the Spirit of Jesus" (2 Corinthians 5:17; Philippians 1:9).

My friend, it is this great gift of the Holy Spirit that gives you the ability to live a godly life. The Holy Spirit gives you and your husband (if he is a believer) all of the spiritual resources you both need to have God's kind of marriage.

Tapping into God's Power

So the question becomes this: How can you and your husband tap into this internal spiritual power? That's where our verse to pray comes in. Look again at Galatians 5:16 in your Bible or on the first page of this chapter. Get it into your heart and mind, and then we will see what it means and how we can put it to use in our commitment to pray for our husbands. Based on our verse, here is a sample prayer you can use each day:

My Prayer for My Husband
Galatians 5:16

Dear Lord, I pray that _____ will submit to and be guided by the Holy Spirit today and every day. May he be led moment by moment throughout his day as he makes decisions. Guard and enable _____ not to give in to the desires of the flesh, but to walk by the Spirit.

As you read and pray this verse, remember its source. The apostle Paul wrote these words. He had just presented, one verse earlier, a picture of what happens when Christians fail to love or serve one another: "If you bite and devour one another, beware lest you be consumed by one another!" That is a scary word picture of a pack of wild animals viciously attacking and killing each other. This ugly picture illustrates what happens when believers fail to turn to God and rely upon His Spirit's power—what happens when we allow our sinful nature to take control. So what is the solution? Notice these elements in this one verse.

The command—"Walk." Think again about the effort it takes for Jim and me to maintain our apple tree so it will bear fruit. Well, "walk" is a command by God to His people to make an effort—to do something! When sin lies at your door, you have a choice. You can lie, sit, or stand there and do nothing about it. Or you can walk. To walk refers to movement, action, direction, effort. In what direction should you and your husband be moving?

The direction—"...in the Spirit." As a believer, you have another choice you can make—you can choose which way you will walk. Paul is saying you should move in the realm or influence of the Holy Spirit. It's another way to describe being filled with the Spirit. When you walk in the Spirit, you are choosing to obey God and His commands. You are choosing to let Him influence your direction—to be controlled by the Spirit and do what God wants you to do. When you walk in the Spirit, you have God's Holy Spirit guiding and instructing you. He is helping, enabling, and empowering you to act correctly and make the right decisions. Your feet are on the right path as you tackle your day filled with the Spirit.

This, my fellow prayer warrior, is what you are praying will occur in your husband's heart too—that he will "walk in the Spirit."

The alternative—"...you shall not fulfill the lust of the flesh." It's a fact of life—there is a battle going on inside you. The battle is between the Spirit and your old self—your sinful human nature, what Paul calls "the lust of the flesh." In verse 17, Paul describes this conflict: "The flesh sets its desire against the Spirit, and the Spirit against the flesh; for these are in opposition to one another, so that you may not do the things that you please" (NASB).

Once again, you have a choice. When you choose to obey

God and walk in the Spirit, you will not fulfill the lust of the flesh. Instead, you will exhibit what is called the fruit of the Spirit. This supernatural fruit, or behavior, is described in verses 22-23.

The Fruit of the Spirit

Throughout the Bible, the word "fruit" refers to evidence of what is within. Any person who has received Jesus as Savior has the Lord living inside, and that indwelling presence of Jesus' Spirit will reveal itself as good "fruit"—the "fruits of righteousness" (Philippians 1:11). Take a look at a few brief facts about the fruit of the Spirit:

— Godly spiritual behavior is expressed as love, joy, peace, patience, kindness, goodness, faithfulness, gentleness, and self-control.

— Every fruit of the Spirit is commanded in Scripture: "Walk by the Spirit" (Galatians 5:16).

— Every fruit, because each is commanded, requires a decision, a choice. Will you or won't you walk in the Spirit? If you choose to do so, "you shall not fulfill the lust of the flesh" (Galatians 5:16).

— Every fruit of the Spirit is illustrated and seen in the life of Christ. Walking by the Spirit means being controlled by the Spirit. It means acting like Jesus. Jesus walked moment by moment in and by the Spirit. Therefore, His life habitually and totally exhibited godly behavior. He lived in constant joy, He loved perfectly, etc.

This godly behavior—the fruit of the Spirit—is what you and your husband can expect to see in each other when you are walking with Jesus and living like Jesus.

Are you wondering, "What if my husband isn't a Christian?" If he isn't, he does not know Jesus and what He is like. But your husband knows *you* and can see *you*—and *Jesus in you*! When you walk in the Spirit, you act and respond like Christ, and your husband can't miss it. Yes, you will pray and pray—and pray for your husband's salvation. And you will also pray for yourself, that you will show him, through your life, how Jesus would act if He were living under the same roof with you and your husband. You show your husband your Redeemer by showing him your redeemed life.

Walking by the Spirit

If your husband is a Christian, I hope you praise God with your every waking breath! Both Jim and I have seen—and experienced—the strain that occurs in a marriage in which one spouse isn't a believer. In fact, we were that couple for the first eight years of our marriage.

Beyond praising God each day that your husband is in Christ, pray that he too will submit to the power of the indwelling Spirit and be an imitator of Christ.

When you and your husband are walking by the Spirit, you will both exhibit the following fruit of the Spirit:

The fruit of love—Love is self-sacrifice. This simple definition crystalizes what the Bible teaches about love. "Love is not an emotion. It is an act of sacrificing self. It is not necessarily feeling love toward a particular person. It may not have any emotion connected with it."[1] God's kind of love is not the love portrayed by the world. The world's kind of love is a basic emotion, while the Bible describes love this way: "God demonstrates His own love toward us, in that while we were still sinners, Christ died for us" (Romans 5:8). In this verse we sense no emotion, but we certainly see that God's love involved the greatest sacrifice any person can make.

This is a book about loving your husband enough to pray for him. In fact, the first person who should receive the overflow of your love for God and your prayers to God is your husband.

Healthy positive emotions contribute to a healthy marriage, but God's kind of love goes beyond the external and superficial. The world's kind of love is conditional: "If you love me, then I'll love you." It's transitory: "I don't love you anymore." Or, "I've fallen out of love with you." By contrast, God's kind of love is unconditional: "I love you regardless."

When a husband (or a wife) is walking by the Spirit, his love is enduring, unwavering, impartial, and willing to sacrifice for the good of you and his children. When your husband is Spirit-filled, his love will be shown in his actions. And that's what you are praying for!

> ❧ **A Pause for Prayer** ❧
>
> *Father of all love, I pray _____'s love for You and our family will manifest itself in his willingness to be a daily, living sacrifice as he gives his time and effort to his family.*

The fruit of joy—When life is good and things are going well at home and problems are few and far between, praise and thanksgiving flow freely from your heart and lips. When the sun is shining brightly on your life, you are happy. But when life turns black and stormy, praise and thanksgiving don't flow quite so easily. This is where people often become confused about the difference between spiritual joy and the emotion of happiness.

Happiness is an emotion we have when we are experiencing good fortune and success. But you can experience *spiritual joy* even in the most severe trials when you choose to follow God's advice and "in everything give thanks; for this is the will of God in Christ Jesus for you" (1 Thessalonians 5:18).

This is why a more accurate definition of joy is that joy is the "sacrifice" of praise. Like love, joy is a sacrifice. Even when you don't feel like praising the Lord or thanking Him, you do what God says, and in spite of your circumstances, you seek joy. At times when you would rather bask in self-pity or stay stuck in depression, you choose to look beyond your pain and make your praise a sacrifice to God. As Hebrews 13:15 says, "Let us continually offer the sacrifice of praise to God, that is, the fruit of our lips, giving thanks to His name."

A Pause for Prayer

Father of all joy, I pray that _____ will walk through his day filled with the Spirit's joy, regardless of what happens in his life today. I pray that our marriage and home will reflect the joy of the Lord...no matter what.

The fruit of peace—Peace is the sacrifice of trust. You and I make this sacrifice when we face pain and stress and choose to trust God instead of panicking or falling apart or getting angry. When circumstances might tempt you to panic, feel terrified, or become a nervous wreck, you can either give in to those feelings or trust in God. You can present yourself to Him and be filled with His peace, or you can succumb to the emotions of the flesh. It's your choice.

Your prayer is that your husband will choose to trust God—choose to make the sacrifice of trust. This will cause him to experience God's peace even in the midst of tremendous chaos. The apostle Paul described the sacrifice of trust this way:

> Be anxious for nothing, but in everything by prayer and supplication, with thanksgiving, let your requests be made known to God; and the peace of God, which surpasses all understanding, will guard your hearts and minds through Christ Jesus (Philippians 4:6-7).

A Pause for Prayer

Father of all peace, I ask You to make _____ a rock of calm strength regardless of what might be happening to him and to us, his family. I pray that _____ will trust You to give him the wisdom, knowledge, and peace he needs to accomplish what You are asking of him. Help _____ as a husband and father to trust in Your grace and enjoy the peace only You can give.

The fruit of patience—As with the other fruit of the Spirit, you and I are called by God to be patient. God's Word instructs us to "put on...patience" (Colossians 3:12 NASB). Patience is choosing to "do nothing" until you check in with God and know the right thing to do. Patience has the ability to wait and wait and wait some more...for a very long time, if necessary.

Patience is in short supply in many marriages. And so you pray! You pray for patience, especially when God seems to be taking His time with changing your husband. But also realize how patient God is with you when you resist His efforts to change you.

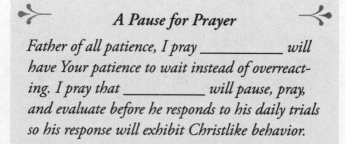

A Pause for Prayer

Father of all patience, I pray _____ will have Your patience to wait instead of overreacting. I pray that _____ will pause, pray, and evaluate before he responds to his daily trials so his response will exhibit Christlike behavior.

The fruit of kindness—While patience waits and does nothing sinful, like get mad, yell, or storm off, kindness plans for godly action, for a godly response. Kindness chooses to "do something." It *chooses* to do something constructive. This may not sound very special, but Spirit-filled kindness is genuine, warm-hearted concern for other people—the kind Jesus had for others, which makes it exquisite and extremely important. It is a matter of the heart. Therefore, do as Colossians 3:12 advises and "put on" kindness. Clothe yourself with God's kindness.

> ❧　　　***A Pause for Prayer***　　❧
>
> *Father of all kindness, I pray _____will*
> *demonstrate Your kindness and concern for the*
> *welfare of others, including his family.*

The fruit of goodness—Goodness will "do everything" it can to shower God's blessings upon others. Goodness follows through on the concerns of kindness—it takes the giant step from good intentions to actually doing everything it can to serve others. John Wesley, the famous preacher of several centuries ago, understood this principle of doing everything. In fact, he chose to make it a rule for his life, and put the following words into practice:

> Do all the good you can,
> by all the means you can,
> in all the ways you can,
> in all the places you can,
> in all the times you can,
> to all the people you can,
> as long as ever you can.

> ❧　　　***A Pause for Prayer***　　❧
>
> *Father of all goodness, remind _____*
> *today of Your goodness to us. Put him on high*
> *alert today to do all the good he can in all the*
> *ways he can.*

The fruit of faithfulness—The solid fruit of faithfulness means choosing to *do it*...no matter what. To *do it*—whatever "it" is that needs to be done—regardless of feelings, moods, or desires. *Do it!* must become your couple battle cry as the two of you struggle each day with faithfulness and follow through on your many responsibilities. Sure, you and you husband probably have different areas of weakness. Tiredness may head the list...followed closely by laziness, maybe even a dash of indifference. But when you make a decision to *do it* and look to God for His strength and purpose in *doing it*, He gives you the grace you need to have victory over any obstacle that stands between you and doing what's right, doing God's will.

> ❧   *A Pause for Prayer*   ❧
>
> *Father of all faithfulness, I realize this trait is
> one of Your attributes. I pray _____ will
> choose to be faithful to You in his walk with You,
> and faithful to fulfill his roles as husband, father,
> and provider along with all his many other
> responsibilities today.*

The fruit of gentleness—Gentleness, or "meekness" as it is sometimes translated, like the other fruit of the Spirit, requires you to trust God. Gentleness chooses to "take it." Gentleness doesn't mean weakness. It actually has the idea of "strength under control."

A husband who is characterized by gentleness finds refuge in the Lord and His ways. This enables him to endure unkind behavior and suffering by trusting in the provision and purposes of an all-wise and caring Father. In the eyes of the world, gentleness may look like weakness, but choosing to exhibit this fruit calls for the greatest of strength!

And for those sticky situations you face in your day that could easily evoke some very nongentle responses from you, look to God for guidance. If you run up against the same problem day after day (like a child that keeps misbehaving or a husband who is perpetually angry), look to God for guidance *and* seek counsel from others. Whatever you do, keep your eyes on the Lord, and He will lead you in the paths of righteousness (Psalm 23:3).

> ❧   *A Pause for Prayer*   ☙
>
> *Father of all gentleness, I pray that _____ will trust You for what is happening in his life today. If _____ encounters a tough issue today, help him remember to look to You for Your gentleness. Remind him to trust in Your knowledge of the situation and Your watch-care over him.*

The fruit of self-control—In times of temptation a Christian who walks by the Spirit chooses to remember "Don't do it!" In other words, you and your husband don't give in to wrong emotions, cravings, or urges. You choose not to think or do what you know is wrong. God's fruit of the Spirit self-control gives you the power to say *no* to your flesh—no to food, thoughts, behaviors, sexual struggles, and every other sin that goes against God's will.

> ❧   *A Pause for Prayer*   ❧
>
> *Father of all self-control, please give _____*
> *the resolve to say no to any behavior that would*
> *dishonor Christ and harm _____ and*
> *our family in any way. Help _____ to*
> *walk in Your ways, to be controlled by Your*
> *Spirit.*

The Art of Walking

Love, joy, peace, patience, kindness, goodness, faithfulness, gentleness, and self-control. What a beautiful life—and marriage—you and your husband will experience when these elements of God's grace are at the center of your daily lives. Even if your husband is not a Christian, he and your entire family will be blessed when *you* are careful to walk in the Spirit.

In simple terms, walking by the Spirit means living each moment in submission to God. It means seeking to please God with the thoughts you choose to think, the words you choose to say, and the actions you choose to take. Walking by the Spirit means obediently letting God guide you each step of the way. It's submitting to Him so He works within you.

Unfortunately, walking by the Spirit isn't easy. I'm sure you've noticed that even though you have been born again by the renewing work of the Spirit, you still struggle with sin. And to compound the problem, you have a husband you are bound to physically and legally and in God's eyes who also struggles with sin. As his wife, you cannot play the role of the Holy Spirit in his life. That is impossible—and besides that, it is not your responsibility. It's God's!

But you can faithfully and fervently pray for him. Pray for your husband to know and love God, and to walk in His Spirit. And pray that you would walk in the Spirit and be filled by Him minute-by-minute as you respond to your minute-by-minute challenges by doing what God teaches in the Bible. And as you do so, trust God with your husband's heart and growth.

And now for the big question: How do you walk with God?

> One foot in front of the other
> One thought at a time
> One sentence at a time
> One response at a time
> One decision at a time
> One minute at a time
> One day at a time
> And when you fail, stop it,
> admit it, confess it, apologize for it, and go on.

A Prayer to Pray from the Heart of Paul

Philippians 1:9

*This I pray, that your love may abound
still more and more in knowledge
and all discernment.*

Chapter 14

Praying for Your Husband to Be a Leader

*The husband is head of the wife, as
also Christ is head of the church.*

EPHESIANS 5:23

It's hard to imagine, but marriage was not man's invention. No, it was all God's idea. In fact, marriage was the first institution God established with the first couple ever, Adam and Eve. In them He formed the perfect team. Together they were told to rule the world. They were to be a unified and indivisible force. However, with the entrance of sin into the world, the Adam and Eve team became fractured as each brought their self-interests into the marriage. From that point in time onward, leadership within marriages has been a hotly debated subject—and a hot topic in many marriages!

Hundreds of centuries later, the New Testament book of Ephesians gave us wives a verse we can use to pray for our husbands. At a time when the institution of marriage was in severe trouble, not only in the Jewish community but also in Greek and Roman societies, the apostle Paul presented some revolutionary instructions for fulfilling God's design for marriage.

And amazingly, what Paul wrote in Ephesians is still revolutionary for our world today! He said that a Christian marriage will function best if the husband is the leader. Quite a concept, right?

God's Winning Formula

I've been sharing throughout this book that I lived...no, I survived...28 years of living without a set of working guidelines for life. Then, as a new Christian who had failed miserably as a wife for 8 years, I wanted to know exactly what it was that God wanted me to know, to be, and to do. So I dug into my new Bible to find out what it said about my role as a wife. As I read, I noticed that God's plan was really quite simple—and very clear. God's foundation for marriage is found in your verse to pray for your husband. Take a minute to read the verse on the first page of this chapter.

My Prayer for My Husband
Ephesians 5:23

Dear Lord, I pray that You will strengthen and enable _____ to own his role as the head of our marriage as Jesus owned His role as head of the church. Guide _____ and give him Your wisdom. Strengthen his faith and trust in You as he leads us as a couple and a family with love and purpose.

Paradise Lost

In the beginning and for all time thereafter, there has been only one perfect marriage. That was between Adam and Eve. It was perfect because there was no sin. God, being sinless, could only create what was pure and sinless. Therefore, Adam and Eve were pure and sinless. Can you imagine the joy and harmony this couple experienced 24/7? No arguments. No snide remarks. No struggles with decision making. Each and every day was utterly perfect. Pure bliss and zero stress. Never a moment of fear or disappointment. No money worries. Oh, and no in-law problems! Ahhh...sweet!

We don't know how long this privileged couple had before the world of sin came crashing down around them. From the point of the first conniving attack by "the serpent"[1] on Eve and the couple's ensuing defeat, our enemy Satan has been using the same successful strategy to attack and destroy marriages. And he's got plenty of everyday help from our selfish sin nature, which does an adequate job of keeping marriage partners at odds with each other.

Here's how things went in Genesis 3 with Adam and Eve. As you read along, keep reminding yourself that the same actions and attitudes occur in marriages today, including yours.

Blaming one another or others—A natural response to problems is for each partner to blame the other for what happened. In the perfect Garden of Eden, the serpent tempted Eve to eat the fruit God has expressly forbidden her and Adam to eat. In fact, it was the *only* thing Adam and Eve were not to do! Well, you know the story: Eve ate the fruit...and then gave the fruit to Adam...who ate the fruit as well (Genesis 3:6).

When God called Adam, Eve, and the serpent together after

the fall into sin had occurred, the blame worked its way right back up the chain:

- Adam blamed Eve, saying, "The woman whom You gave to be with me, she gave me of the tree, and I ate" (verse 12).

- Eve then blamed the serpent: "The serpent deceived me, and I ate" (verse 13).

Neither Adam nor Eve took responsibility for their actions. Each looked around to see where they could place the blame.

And unfortunately, the blaming still goes on today. Neither partner wants to shoulder any of the blame when things go wrong. And this is where leadership in a marriage caves in.

My husband, Jim, has been writing to men on the topic of leadership for many years, and he believes that Adam should have stepped up and taken responsibility for what happened. Adam was responsible for Eve. Notice that God summoned and addressed Adam about what the two of them had done—not Eve: "Then the Lord called to Adam and said to him..." (verse 9).

The battle of the sexes began and continues—We don't know what might have happened if Adam had taken leadership and responsibility, but according to Scripture, God then judged this threesome and meted out their punishment. Things would never be the same in the world or in Adam and Eve's marital relationship. Read on to see what happened:

So the Lord God said to the serpent: "Because you have done this, you are cursed more than all cattle, and more than every beast of the field; on your belly you shall go, and you shall eat dust all the days of your life. And I will put enmity between you and the woman, and between your seed and her Seed; He shall bruise your head, and you shall bruise His heel" (verses 14-15).

To the woman God said, "Your desire shall be for your husband, and he shall rule over you" (verse 16).

Then to Adam He said:

> Because you have heeded the voice of your wife, and have eaten from the tree of which I commanded you, saying, "You shall not eat of it": Cursed is the ground for your sake; in toil you shall eat of it all the days of your life. Both thorns and thistles it shall bring forth for you, and you shall eat the herb of the field. In the sweat of your face you shall eat bread till you return to the ground, for out of it you were taken; for dust you are, and to dust you shall return (verses 17-19).

Commenting on the results of the fall and Adam and Eve's sin, one theologian notes:

> Because of sin and the curse, the man and the woman will face struggles in their own relationship. Sin has turned the harmonious system of God-ordained roles into distasteful struggles of self-will. Lifelong companions, husbands and wives, will need God's help in getting along as a result. The woman's desire will be to lord it over her husband, but the husband will rule by divine design.[2]

So What's Next?

Have you ever lost an expensive pair of earrings and spent hours searching for them? I'm guessing you didn't give up until you found them, right? Well, think about this: How much more important is your marriage? Earrings are *things*—things that can be replaced. But your marriage? Your husband? Well, that's another story.

When it comes to your marriage, you should be willing to do whatever it takes to produce God's kind of marriage relationship. You should commit to following His rules and guidelines, to living out His will for you and your spouse. God has placed you in your marriage and expects you to do your part. That's His will for *you*. And, to be sure, God has His guidelines for your husband too. But He only asks *you* to focus on and take care of *your* role.

So we wonder: *How do wives do this? How can I as a wife do this?*

A good principle to remember is this: When something looks impossible to do or seems hopeless, go back to the Bible and review what God says. This always helps. With a prayer in your heart, revisit the biblical basics. A fresh look at what God's Word says will simplify your problems and give you answers. Solomon, the wisest man of his day, instructed, "In all your ways acknowledge Him, and He shall direct your paths" (Proverbs 3:6). And, my all-time favorite verse about trusting and committing to doing what the Bible says is Psalm 33:11: "The counsel of the Lord stands forever, the plans of His heart to all generations."

A Leader Needs a Follower

You can't get any more basic than this truth: "A leader cannot lead unless he has at least one follower." Your husband will have a tough time leading if you aren't willing to follow. Just as you cannot make your husband lead, he cannot make you follow. Therefore, you must choose to submit.

In this chapter, your verse to pray for your husband is Ephesians 5:23: "The husband is head of the wife, as also Christ is head of the church." And the verse that precedes this statement says, "Wives, submit to your own husbands, as to the Lord."

And there it is! The husband is the head—the leader. And the wife is the follower. This is reinforced in Colossians 3:18, a similar verse: "Wives, submit to your own husbands, as is fitting in the Lord." This means that in the same way you are to submit to the Lord, you are to also willingly follow your husband's leadership.

Now let's put verses 22 through 24 together:

²² Wives, submit to your own husbands, as to the Lord.

²³ For the husband is head of the wife, as also Christ is head of the church; and He is the Savior of the body.

²⁴ Therefore, just as the church is subject to Christ, so let the wives be to their own husbands in everything.

The word "submit" is a combination of two words with a military background. It means "to line up, to get in order, to arrange, to rank beneath or under." Later, in verse 33, Paul switched from submission to "respect." Your submission shouldn't be resented or resisted, but seen as an assignment given to you by God Himself. Out of love and respect, you are to commit to following your husband and adapting yourself to his leadership and his way of leading.

Now, before you start reacting to this concept of submission, realize that even though the command here in Ephesians 5 and also in Colossians 3 is specific for your role in your marriage, *all* Christians are to voluntarily submit and arrange themselves under one another as God commands...not over one another (see Philippians 2:3-8).

Here's a thought: Don't you think it's interesting to notice that God did not tell husbands to lead, but directed His communication to wives—to you? He's letting you know that you are to follow your husband as he leads.

How Not to Follow God's Plan

Do you know how some wives follow God's plan? They become husband-watchers. (Hopefully you are not one of them!) They know all about what God says their husband is supposed to do and be, and they know how God instructs and expects husbands to treat their wives. But instead of praying for God to change their husband and earnestly focusing on taking care of their own faithfulness to their God-given assignments as wives, they try to take on the self-appointed role of playing "Holy Spirit."

This kind of wife believes it is her duty to point out her husband's faults and shortcomings. She may even assume a "when...then" attitude. In her heart (and maybe even verbally), she decides, "When he does this or that, then I'll do this or that." She postpones obedience to her role as a wife and makes submitting to her husband's leadership conditional to her husband's behavior.

Following God's Plan by Praying—and Looking Up

There is hope and help for all of us...and it's prayer! The Bible tells us:

- If anyone lacks wisdom, look up—let him ask of God.
- If anyone lacks love or patience or self-control, look up—do what God says and walk by the Spirit.

When you stop what you are doing or thinking that goes against God's Word, when you stop in your tracks or stop your diatribe and pray, that's looking up. That's checking in with God and checking yourself and your words and behavior. That's you looking to God to help you with your husband, to supply you with His wisdom, His love, His patience, and His self-control.

In this chapter we are focusing specifically on you praying that your husband will lead in your marriage. And what you are praying for won't happen overnight. Praying for your husband's leadership in your marriage and family is a lifelong assignment from the Lord. And here are a few key ways that you can pray:

Pray for your husband to lead by loving—The world's concept of leadership is lordship. Many men (and this may include your husband) were raised in a home where the husband dominated. He led by intimidation. As a result, maybe your husband doesn't know any other model to follow. To review, in Ephesians 5, husbands are commanded, "Love your wives, just as Christ also loved the church and gave Himself for her" (verse 25). Your husband's leadership is to be demonstrated not in lording it over you and the children, but in love—in his willingness to sacrifice his time, money, and life for you and the kids. What wife wouldn't willingly follow and submit to a man who is prepared to sacrifice everything for her and their family?

Pray for your husband to give you spiritual guidance—This means you are basically praying he will read his Bible, go to church, be mentored, and be supportive of your desire to grow spiritually mature.

Pray for your husband to pray for you—The greatest way your husband can lead you is to know what's happening in your life, to be clued in to your fears and struggles, your hopes and dreams. This can occur as the two of you talk together and pray for and with each other.

Pray for your husband to lead with understanding—The Bible refers to you, as the wife, as "someone weaker" (1 Peter 3:7 NASB). This is a reference to physical strength, not to mental or spiritual capacities and abilities. First Peter 3:7 instructs, "Husbands...be considerate as you live with your wives, and treat them with respect as the weaker partner and as heirs with you of the gracious gift of life, so that nothing will hinder your prayers" (1 Peter 3:7 NIV).

The fact that you are weaker physically is not meant to reflect on you negatively. It's simply an affirmation of your need for protection and provision. That is the leadership role your husband is to assume. He is to literally "shoulder" more of the physical responsibilities in your lives and your home.

Pray for your husband to lead his children—Biblically speaking and historically, it is the father who, in Christian homes, is the leader in the training of the children. Pray that your husband will...

— take an active role in the children's lives.

— help with the physical, mental, and spiritual nurturing of the children.

— read the Bible with the children and help them memorize key Bible verses.

— pray with the children at meals and as part of the bedtime routine.

But What If...?

At this point you may have some questions. You may be thinking, *But wait a minute. What if my husband...?* Let's look at three "what if" situations many wives find themselves in.

But what if I don't have leadership problems in my marriage? Praise the Lord! You are fortunate and blessed of God. But don't let up on your prayer efforts. The fact that your marriage relationship is going well should cause you to redouble your efforts in praying for your husband and his role as leader. As Peter warned, "Be sober, be vigilant; because your adversary the devil walks about like a roaring lion, seeking whom he may devour" (1 Peter 5:8). Your adversary would love to destroy the strong relationship you and your husband enjoy. Do your part to keep your marriage on track by praying and by living out God's roles for you as a wife.

Be proactive! Redouble your efforts in supporting your husband. Let him know how much you appreciate his leadership. Tell him you are praying for him every day as he leads and loves his family. Keep checking with him for any concerns he has on the job, and pray faithfully for his wisdom and discernment as he handles them. Make sure you are always looking for ways to support his leadership in front of the children.

But what if I am married to a passive Christian? This type of husband definitely needs your prayers. This is the husband who, when you ask for guidance, responds with, "It's up to you, honey." Or "Whatever you want, babe." Or, "It doesn't matter to me. You make that call."

Again, your first priority is to pray. Beyond that, your role still stands: You are to help, follow, respect, and love your mate. Make it a goal to learn better ways of asking for direction and for discussing the issues that face your marriage and family. Put the brakes on any behavior that is producing negative results. Guard your heart against frustration and guard your mouth against criticism. Most of all, guard against taking over the leadership in your home.

Granted, when your husband is gone from home for work or on deployment, you must step in and fill the leadership gap. But when your husband is home, find ways to ask him to make the decisions, to give directions, to function as the leader. As you interact daily, keep in mind what we learned earlier—that two wrongs don't make a right. Your husband's failure to lead does not mean you must rush in and lead. Adjust and experiment with new and better ways of communicating with your husband so he, in time, becomes the leader in your household. And I just can't say it enough: Pray! Pray a thousand times a day, if you must.

But what if I'm married to a man who is not a Christian? God's Word and your roles still stand in your marriage. Your job assignment from God is not to change your husband, and it's not to save him. Salvation through Christ and real change occur by a divine, supernatural work that only God can accomplish in your husband's heart.

So above all else, keep on praying. And keep on doing what you know God expects of you and every wife who is a Christian—to help, follow, respect, and love. Make it a goal to assist and minister to your non-Christian husband in as many ways you can think of. Open your heart and mouth and praise him for what he does do for you and your family. Look for his many good qualities and let him know how much you appreciate him—daily!

Also, you cannot expect a husband who is not a Christian

to act like a man who is. So be careful not to compare him with Christian husbands. Remember too that God can help you do anything, including loving your unbelieving husband. Or as a friend of mine referred to her unbelieving husband, your "beloved unbeliever."

Counting on God's Care

Wherever life finds you today, don't be discouraged. Don't give in to depression, despair, defeat, doubt, or dismay. Take heart! God knows your situation and your heart. Your God is the same God who, when speaking to Moses about the bondage of the Israelites in Egypt, said...

>...He had *heard* the cries of the people.
>
>...He had *seen* their oppression.
>
>...He had *come down*, and
>
>...He was *doing something about it!*
>
>*He was sending Moses* (see Exodus 3:9-10).

You must trust God to do His part in your life, your husband's life, and your marriage. Count on the fact that God *knows* all about your situation. He knows *everything!* He knows whether your husband is a believer or not, whether your husband is a great leader or hesitant to take on that role. And He knows every single desire of your heart and every heartfelt concern you have for your husband, your marriage, and your relationship with him.

Count on the fact and the truth that God cares about your situation and your marriage, and He cares about it even more than you do.

And so you pray! Pray to be God's kind of wife in the marriage

you have today. Pray that your husband will love Christ and grow
to love Him even more. Pray that your man, as the head of your
home, will take charge of your marriage and be the husband
and leader God wants him to be. And while you are praying,

> wait on the LORD;
> be of good courage,
> and He shall strengthen your heart;
> wait, I say, on the LORD! (Psalm 27:14).

❧ ⸻ ••⊙•• ⸻ ❧

Advice on Prayer from the Heart of Jesus
Matthew 6:6

> *When you pray, go into your room,*
> *and when you have shut your door,*
> *pray to your Father who is in the secret place;*
> *and your Father who sees in secret*
> *will reward you openly.*

Chapter 15

Praying for Your Husband as a Team Player

*Two are better than one, because they have
a good reward for their labor. For if they
fall, one will lift up his companion.*

ECCLESIASTES 4:9-10

e have come a long way in discovering what it means to be praying for our husbands, haven't we? Basically we have been moving forward and putting together a composite of what a husband's priorities look like. When these priorities are lived out, it makes for one amazing guy! And if I'm not mistaken, as you started and are continuing to pray, your husband is beginning to look and act more like that guy, if he isn't already!

The infusion of God's Word into your life, and your understanding and attention to your own role as a wife, are probably having a noticeable effect on your behavior, your outlook, and your thoughts concerning your marriage and your husband. My respect for you is sky high for staying with me through our study of so many incredible scriptures, along with some repetition and review. Well done, my reading friend! As the saying goes, the hardest step of any change or project is getting started.

I'm congratulating you for getting started. After all, you've made it to the end of this book. Some things in life are repeated daily—forever. And one of these things is definitely praying for your husband. It should be a lifelong desire and focus, and by God's grace, it will be yours.

But before we close out our time together, I have one more verse I want you to use in prayer. You'll like it because it focuses on being best friends with your hubby! It's a verse and prayer about your husband being a team player as the two of you work together on the day-in, day-out functioning of your marriage.

Now let's see for ourselves the impact and productivity that can result from a marriage in which the spouses work as a team. Meet Aquila and Priscilla, a "power couple" in the Bible, a couple who worked successfully in tandem. This couple will be a guide and example you can follow. This is my husband's favorite couple in Scripture, and his desire has always been for the two of us to follow in their footsteps.

But first, a word from the wisest man of his day, King Solomon.

"Two Are Better Than One"

These words were written by King Solomon. Unfortunately, Solomon didn't always live out his counsel to others, but his God-breathed wisdom can still give us direction for our lives today. In Ecclesiastes 4:8-10, Solomon recounted the woes and emptiness experienced by a person who is without companionship. He also said it doesn't have to be that way. Verses 9 and 10 make up our verses to pray. Be sure to read these verses for yourself in your Bible or on the first page of this chapter. Then let's see what they mean.

My Prayer for My Husband
Ecclesiastes 4:9-10

Dear Lord, I pray for _____ to realize that he and I can enjoy greater harmony and accomplish so much more when we work together as a team. May _____ trust me and know in his heart that if he falls, I will be right there to lift him up, and together we two will be better than one.

In these verses, Solomon talked about teamwork in action. He said, "Two are better than one." Solomon then explained what happens when two people refuse to work together or fail to do so: "Woe to him who is alone when he falls, for he has no one to help him up. Again, if two lie down together, they will keep warm; but how can one be warm alone?" (verses 10-11).

Marriage does have many positives, like having a warm body next to you on a cold night! But this idea of being a team is obviously broader than couples seeing their partner as simply being a bed-warmer. How about having someone to talk with after a tough day at work or home? How about having someone to discuss hard decisions with? Or how about (which was really vital to me as a young mother!) having someone—your children's dad—to team up with on how to deal with child-raising issues?

Marriage Is Like a Three-Legged Sack Race

I'm sure you have been at a picnic or a summer camp and participated in, or at least observed, a three-legged sack race. You know the game. Two people each put one leg in a burlap sack, forming a "three-legged" competitor. It's a riot to watch the teams struggle and adjust as they attempt to coordinate their movements so that they can hop their way to the finish line as quickly as possible. Who wins the race? The couple who is best able to work together as a team!

Which brings up the question: How can I work with my husband as a teammate if he hasn't grasped this concept yet?

The first step, as always, is to begin and keep on praying for your husband to see the value of working together in your marriage. This giant first step can then lead to working together as a team with your children, in the church, and in your community. What would such a marriage team look like? For an answer, let's look at Priscilla and Aquila, an amazing couple who worked together as a team.

The Dynamic Duo

We first meet this Jewish couple in Acts 18:2. The year is AD 50. Because all Jews were evicted from Rome, Aquila and Priscilla moved to Corinth. Later, when the apostle Paul arrived in Corinth, he found this couple, who were already Christians. And, like Paul, they were tent makers. It was a perfect fit, and Paul began working alongside the two of them.

This was a phenomenal team who were truly a couple after God's own heart. They presented a model of how effective you and your husband can be when you work together, whether it comes to the care of your family, running a business, working in the church, or being evangelistic lights in your community.

Nothing but positive comments are recorded in the Bible about this dynamic couple. Everywhere they ministered they were a blessing to the locals, to both Christians and non-Christians. Here is a little of their story:

They helped found the church in Corinth. They ministered alongside the apostle Paul while he preached the gospel. The Bible doesn't say, but it's quite possible they did a little preaching as well:

> [Paul] found a certain Jew named Aquila, born in Pontus, who had recently come from Italy with his wife Priscilla (because Claudius had commanded all the Jews to depart from Rome); and he came to them (Acts 18:2).

> Paul still remained a good while. Then he took leave of the brethren and sailed for Syria, and Priscilla and Aquila were with him...And he came to Ephesus, and left them [Priscilla and Aquila] there; but he himself entered the synagogue and reasoned with the Jews (verses 18-19).

They laid the groundwork for the expansion of the church. In Acts 18:26, we see this dynamic duo at work: "So he [Apollos] began to speak boldly in the synagogue. When Aquila and Priscilla heard him, they took him aside and explained to him the way of God more accurately." That is, they realized Apollos was missing some parts of the gospel message. So they invited him over for Sunday lunch and filled in his understanding of God's plan of salvation.

They opened their home to the church at Ephesus. At the end of Paul's first letter to the church at Corinth, he wrote a greeting from this beloved couple, along with those who attended church in their home: "The churches of Asia greet you. Aquila and Priscilla greet you heartily in the Lord, with the church that is in their house" (1 Corinthians 16:19).

They risked their lives in ministry. Later, at the end of his letter to the believers in Rome, Paul sent a special greeting and a tribute to this husband-wife team:

> Greet Priscilla and Aquila, my fellow workers in Christ Jesus, who risked their own necks for my life, to whom not only I give thanks, but also all the churches of the Gentiles. Likewise greet the church that is in their house (Romans 16:3-4).

Only God can measure the powerful contribution this couple made during the formative years of the church! What were their unique qualifications? We might be quick to assume they had lots of theological training, right? But the Bible does not say anything about their education. All we know is that they were simple working folks—tent makers.

I believe Aquila and Priscilla nurtured the kind of unity in their marriage that made it possible for God to use this humble couple in remarkable ways. Together as a couple and as a team, they were simply available—to God, to Paul, to Apollos, and to the people who made up the church. And God used them mightily.

> Teamwork is the fuel that allows common
> people to attain uncommon results.[1]

The Power of Team Effort

Here are just a few observations about Mr. Aquila and Mrs. Priscilla that you can pray about for you and your husband. Even if you cannot pray together, you can be praying yourself about the part you can play in working as a team beside your husband.

They used their spiritual gifts in complete harmony. The names Aquila and Priscilla are never mentioned individually. This astounding couple worked as a team. Yes, you and your husband are each responsible to develop your spiritual gifts, but when you are a team like Aquila and Priscilla were, you have plenty of opportunities to work together in mutual ministry.

They displayed their faith without competition. You might say this couple was "homeschooled." Priscilla and Aquila worked side by side with the apostle Paul, the writer of 13 books of the New Testament. He was not only their friend and associate, but also their resident teacher while they worked together in Corinth. Can you imagine the lively discussions they had each day as they sat together stitching those tents? After several years of this sort of daily interaction and Paul's faithful instruction and training, Priscilla and Aquila surely developed a solid understanding of the Messiah and His mission. After all, look who their teacher and mentor was!

Within this couple there was no competitive spirit when it came to spiritual matters. They were both growing spiritually, both ministering. Maybe that's why their names were often reversed. They seemed to have a tag-team mentality. Sometimes one of them took the lead or had the idea, and other times it was the other. But they were never in competition.

Why not take a page out of their Team Aquila and Priscilla's Playbook? First, make sure you are growing spiritually. And, of course, be praying for your husband's growth as well. Second, pray for opportunities for both of you to serve together, maybe with the children's ministry at your church. Or maybe you can do as Jim and I did, volunteering for setup and cleanup for events at the church. When Jim and I first became a Christian couple, we couldn't do much, but we sure could wash pots and pans after the Easter potluck!

If you have children, think about this advice my husband shares in our parenting classes:

> Modeling is a mighty molder of hearts and minds.
> There is no better way to teach your children about
> loving and serving one another than letting them
> see it practiced by their united parents.[2]

They were of one mind in hospitality. Priscilla and Aquila did something any couple can do. They threw open their doors and made their home available for church ministry. This was how the early church grew at this time in history. There were no church buildings, so evangelism took place as people opened their hearts and homes for outreach and church worship.

Again, think about this for your children:

> There is no better training ground for the faith of
> your children than seeing their parents open the
> doors to their home and participating in a family
> ministry right in their own home![3]

They were equally willing to sacrifice. At the end of the epistle to the Romans, Paul sent greetings to Priscilla and Aquila and commented on their sacrificial service: "Greet Priscilla and Aquila, my fellow workers in Christ Jesus, who risked their own necks for my life, to whom not only I give thanks, but also all the churches of the Gentiles" (Romans 16:3-4).

This ordinary couple was effective in their service because their commitment was to their Savior. They were "fellow workers in Christ Jesus." They were committed to the point they were willing to suffer and "risk their own necks." And notice Paul said this extended to "all the churches of the Gentiles." Priscilla and Aquila gave their all—to all.

At this point in time and in your marriage, God may not be asking you and your husband to risk your lives. But He is definitely asking you to "present your bodies a living sacrifice" (Romans 12:1) each and every day. This not only applies to serving God, but describes your role of selfless service right in your own home—to each other and to your children.

Working on Teamwork

Sadly, as I interact with wives and moms on a daily basis, I hear all too often about dads who are giving over the responsibility of parenting to their wives. Rather than doing the heavy lifting of leading, fathers are expecting their wives to shoulder the burdens of decision making, teaching, training, and disciplining. "Dad" then becomes just a good ol' boy who is there, but not there. He doesn't really have an opinion about much of anything, especially anything that relates to the home or the children. He brings home a paycheck and believes he has therefore fulfilled his responsibility.

I hope this is not a picture of what is going on under your roof and in your marriage. But if it is, you must become what is referred to as a "prayer warrior." Commit to fervently and passionately praying for your husband to assume his rightful place as your family's team leader. Own your mission and ministry of praying for your husband with your every breath. As one of my former pastors often stated, "Every breath you breathe in should become a prayer breathed out." Faithfully pray the verses featured in this book. Pray one verse a day—or pray all of them every day! Entreat your heavenly Father to move and work in your husband's heart.

And pray equally as much for yourself. Pray just as fervently to be God's kind of wife, the kind of wife He presents in the Bible. Pray to be faithful in your roles and responsibilities as stated in Scripture. And pray that you would produce spiritual fruit like love, patience, kindness, and gentleness toward your husband—along with a large dose of self-control for yourself!

Teamwork is not natural for most people. Many have been raised by a single parent and have no model of teamwork. Others had parents who provided poor models. And, no matter what our own upbringing was like, we are all selfish individuals with a mind of our own.

With the Fall, God said husbands and wives would struggle in their relationship with each other (Genesis 3:16). As selfish, sinful people, we want what we want, even at the cost of others and our relationships with others. This is one reason marriages, especially in the early years, are often rocky. Each person wants to do things their way. It's not until you both begin working things out, with lots of give and take, that the marriage starts running more smoothly.

Then, just about the time you get the marriage thing worked out, along comes a child, and the dynamic is changed. Now you've added an additional selfish person to the mix! Which means you and your husband have to learn to work as a team with the new dynamic of parenting.

Togetherness Promotes Teamwork

As time and the years go by, on and on go the changes and challenges in your marital relationship. With that in mind, here are some togetherness practices that will help promote teamwork in your marriage:

Pray together—Prayer is the starting point for everything—including your marriage, whether you pray separately or together, and even if you are the only one who prays. Praying together reminds me of the game of football. I don't know a lot about football, but I know one thing: The players have to huddle together again and again to decide their next play.

Praying is your couple-huddle. You and your husband pray together and ask God for the next play He wants the two of you to run in your ever-changing family. Over time, as you both pray, you will begin to hear each other's heart. Your husband's concerns will become your concerns and vice versa until you are in sync, acting and moving as one.

And what if your husband isn't a Christian or he won't pray with you? Well, there is nothing to stop you from praying. Seek the Lord privately and pray your heart out!

Have devotions together—Prayer and devotions go hand in hand, and this is where many couples falter. But don't despair! If your husband can't or won't pray or have devotions, these are still priority activities for you.

Even if a husband is willing to have devotions, there is another problem many couples and families face: The couple or family is rarely at home at the same time, even for one meal. You know the scene: Your husband works late. Maybe you have a job too. The kids have after-school activities, etc.

Huddle with your husband to see how and when you might have devotions as a family. Always remember that something is better than nothing. Five minutes centering as a family on God is better than zero minutes!

Plan together—Planning will provide guidance for your family in the same way that the rudder of a ship keeps it going the right direction. Your team needs common goals and direction. Planning together for managing the issues you face as a couple, as parents, and as a family will give all of you direction. What about schooling for your children (maybe even for yourself)? What about your finances and purchases? Where should you attend church? As you pool your thoughts and pray, you will be working together—not against each other.

And what if your husband is not a natural-born planner? By all means, don't charge ahead without him. You are aiming at planning *together*, so ask. Ask "Should we do this...or this? What do you think, honey?" Get your husband's input and thoughts on the situation, and then plan accordingly. You honor your husband when you ask, listen, and as much as is possible, incorporate his wishes and direction.

Talk together—Communication is the key to your marriage, and it's also the key to working together. It's that couple-huddle thing again! Planning together means you are talking with each other. And when you talk together, ideas and opinions get shared and there are fewer misunderstandings because you both communicated. You and your husband are able to plan and work the plan because you are talking together.

And what if your husband is the silent type? Don't give up or quit trying to communicate—and don't stop loving and respecting him. You talked when you were dating and engaged, so you know it can be done. Both of your thoughts are needed so you can work together as a team. Then when a problem comes up, it's no problem! All of your problems can be solved, or at least a plan can be developed for solving them, when the two of you communicate.

Parent together—Praying, planning, and talking can help solidify your couple approach to child raising. To be an effective parenting team, you must try to be unified in your approach to discipline. As you talk through your role as parents, ask these questions: What does the Bible say about discipline? What do wise couples at our church say about discipline? When Jim and I were in the throes of raising our children, we had a standing appointment every week (actually a Coke date) to discuss how the week went, how our disciplining worked, and what changes we needed to make. Whew—that time together *really* helped us to head into each new week unified and on the same page in our efforts to train up and discipline our kids well.

Serve together as a family—To get started, simply include your children in your ministry projects. Participate as a family in workdays at the church. Have the kids help you with an open house at Christmas as a neighborhood outreach. A family who serves together bonds together. Your children will see you living out your faith—they will see Christianity as a living reality.

If you aren't already serving now, how do you begin? It all starts with making a choice to serve others, not just your family. Look around for opportunities to help out. Then dive in! Service is a part of God's will.

Have fun together—You and your husband need to make an effort to balance out work and all your other responsibilities by making time for some fun. Plan together and insert some fun times into your schedule. Go on outings to museums. Travel to nearby state and national parks and historical sites. If you have children, set up game nights in your home. Fix and serve fondue, or start some crazy traditions like backward dinners, which start with dessert first. These activities were so much fun they are now favorite pastimes in our two daughters' homes.

Work together—How do you teach your children the importance of work and doing that work unto the Lord? It starts in the home with you and your husband assigning projects for them to do alongside of you. Even from an early age, children should be taught to pick up their toys, clean up their room, and help out around the house or yard. Don't let your kids be spectators while you do all the work. Have them help out as well...and don't forget the ice cream later!

Promoting a Team Mentality

In sports, the team that can't work together is the team that loses. A good coach will promote a team spirit and do what is necessary to encourage teamwork. That's what you want in your marriage as well. Try these three simple steps for encouraging your husband to join the team—to be a team player, or even the team leader!

1. Feed him. Ask questions and share suggestions on ways the two of you can work together on a project, and of course let him lead! A marriage partnership is like a dance team. You both cannot lead. Let him lead and you follow, smiling up at him the whole time.

2. Encourage him. Anytime people start something new they will experience hesitation and insecurity. As your husband ventures out as team leader, be careful not to dampen his enthusiasm with negative comments and resistance. Offer a very few suggestions, and be willing to support his choices and his leadership.

3. Be interested in him. Take active interest in your husband's ideas and initiative. Make it a habit to stop what you are doing, turn to him, and really listen when he tells you what he's thinking. It might not be what or how you

would do things, but who knows? Give it a try. It's his idea, and he's leading. As I said, give it a try.

Beyond Praying, What Can You Do?

We've covered a lot of suggestions, ideas, and actions you can take to help build your marriage into a solid, united together team. And, of course, you already know the value of prayer. So what else can you do?

The most important thing you can do for your marriage is determine that you want to be a good wife, the kind of wife God presents in the Bible. Write it down. Make it your goal in life. Then set it before you each day as, in prayer, you once again purpose to embrace, own, live, and master your roles and responsibilities as a wife.

And then you pray—for your dearly beloved husband! Determine you will pray daily, faithfully, and fervently for your husband to assume his rightful place as team leader.

An Affirmation from the Heart of Joshua
Joshua 24:15

*Choose for yourselves this day
whom you will serve...
But as for me and my house,
we will serve the LORD.*

Notes

Answering God's Call to Pray

1. A.A. Milne, "Vespers," from *When We Were Very Young* (New York: E.P. Dutton and Co., date unknown).

2. William Law, *A Practical Treatise Upon Christian Perfection* (London: William and John Innys, 1726), p. 459.

3. George Müller as cited in Nick Harrison, *Power in the Promises* (Grand Rapids: Zondervan, 2013), p. 226.

Chapter 1—Praying for Your Husband's Spiritual Growth

1. William Law, as cited by Sherwood Eliot Wirt, *Topical Encyclopedia of Living Quotations* (Minneapolis: Bethany House, 1982), p. 182.

2. Titus 2:4; Ephesians 5:33; Genesis 2:18 respectively.

3. *Life Application Bible* (Wheaton, IL: Tyndale House and Youth for Christ/USA, 1988), p. 1922.

4. Matthew Henry, *Matthew Henry's Commentary on the Whole Bible, complete and unabridged in one volume* (Peabody, MA: Hendrickson Publishers 2003), p. 2330.

Chapter 2—Praying for Your Marriage

1. Genesis 2:18; Ephesians 5:22,33; Titus 2:4.

Chapter 3—Praying for Your Husband as a Father

·1. Jim George, *A Dad After God's Own Heart* (Eugene, OR: Harvest House, 2014), p. 96.

2. George, *A Dad After God's Own Heart*, p. 105.

Chapter 5—Praying for Your Husband's Job

1. Elizabeth George, *Loving God with All Your Mind* (Eugene, OR: Harvest House, 1994 and 2005).

2. Patrick of Ireland, as cited in Sherwood Eliot Wirt, *Topical Encyclopedia of Living Quotations* (Minneapolis: Bethany House Publishers, 1982), p. 182.

Chapter 6—Praying for Your Husband's View of Money

1. See 1 Timothy 3:3; Titus 1:7; 1 Peter 5:2.

2. Norman Grubb, *C.T Studd, Cricketer and Pioneer* (Fort Washington, PA: CLC Publishers, 2001), pp. 66-67.

3. Elizabeth George, *Prayers to Calm Your Heart* (Eugene, OR: Harvest House, 2014), p. 51.

Chapter 8—Praying for Your Husband's Health

1. Ephesians 6:18; Philippians 1:4; 1 Thessalonians 5:17; 2 Thessalonians 1:11.
2. George Müller, as cited in D.L. Moody, *Notes from My Bible* (Grand Rapids: Baker, 1979), p. 159.

Chapter 9—Praying for Your Husband's Use of Time

1. See pages 69-81 in Jim George, *A Leader After God's Own Heart* (Eugene, OR: Harvest House, 2012).
2. Elizabeth George, *Life Management for Busy Women* (Eugene, OR: Harvest House, 2002, 2014).

Chapter 11—Praying for Your Husband's Speech

1. Acts 16:14; 2 Corinthians 5:18; Psalm 51:10.
2. Norman Wright, *Communication: Key to Your Marriage* (Minneapolis: Bethany House Publishers, 2000).
3. Author unknown.

Chapter 12—Praying for Your Husband to Act with Courage

1. Martin Brecht, *Martin Luther*, trans. James L. Schaaf (Philadelphia: Fortress Press, 1985-93), 1:460.
2. John F. Kennedy, *Profiles in Courage*, inaugural edition (New York: Harper & Row, 1955).
3. Jim George, *What God Wants to Do for You* (Eugene, OR: Harvest House, 2004), p. 48.

Chapter 13—Praying for Your Husband's Walk with God

1. John MacArthur, *Liberty in Christ* (Panorama City, CA: Word of Grace Communications, 1986), p. 88.

Chapter 14—Praying for Your Husband to Be a Leader

1. Also referred to in the Bible as accuser, devil, Satan, deceiver, evil one, tempter, father of lies, liar, and wicked one.
2. John MacArthur, *The MacArthur Study Bible* (Nashville: Word, 1979), p. 21.

Chapter 15—Praying for Your Husband as a Team Player

1. This statement is often attributed to Andrew Carnegie.
2. Adapted from Jim George, *A Dad After God's Own Heart* (Eugene, OR: Harvest House, 2014), p. 149.
3. George, *A Dad After God's Own Heart*, p. 149.

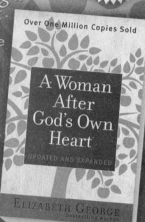
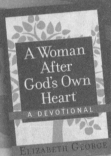

Books by Elizabeth George

- 15 Verses to Pray for Your Husband
- Beautiful in God's Eyes
- Beautiful in God's Eyes for Young Women
- Breaking the Worry Habit...Forever
- Finding God's Path Through Your Trials
- Following God with All Your Heart
- The Heart of a Woman Who Prays
- Life Management for Busy Women
- Loving God with All Your Mind
- Loving God with All Your Mind DVD and Workbook
- A Mom After God's Own Heart
- A Mom After God's Own Heart Devotional
- Moments of Grace for a Woman's Heart
- One-Minute Inspirations for Women
- Prayers to Calm Your Heart
- Quiet Confidence for a Woman's Heart
- Raising a Daughter After God's Own Heart
- The Remarkable Women of the Bible
- Small Changes for a Better Life
- Walking with the Women of the Bible
- A Wife After God's Own Heart
- A Woman After God's Own Heart®—Daily Devotional
- A Woman's Daily Walk with God
- A Woman's Guide to Making Right Choices
- A Woman's High Calling
- A Woman's Walk with God
- A Woman Who Reflects the Heart of Jesus
- A Young Woman After God's Own Heart
- A Young Woman After God's Own Heart—A Devotional
- A Young Woman's Guide to Discovering Her Bible
- A Young Woman's Guide to Making Right Choices
- A Young Woman's Guide to Prayer
- A Young Woman Who Reflects the Heart of Jesus

Study Guides

- Beautiful in God's Eyes
  Growth & Study Guide
- Finding God's Path Through Your Trials
  Growth & Study Guide
- Following God with All Your Heart
  Growth & Study Guide
- Life Management for Busy Women
  Growth & Study Guide
- Loving God with All Your Mind
  Growth & Study Guide
- Loving God with All Your Mind
  Interactive Workbook
- A Mom After God's Own Heart
  Growth & Study Guide
- The Remarkable Women of the Bible
  Growth & Study Guide
- Small Changes for a Better Life
  Growth & Study Guide
- A Wife After God's Own Heart
  Growth & Study Guide
- A Woman After God's Own Heart®
  Growth & Study Guide
- A Woman Who Reflects the Heart of Jesus
  Growth & Study Guide

Children's Books

- A Girl After God's Own Heart
- A Girl After God's Own Heart Devotional
- A Girl's Guide to Discovering Her Bible
- A Girl's Guide to Making Really Good Choices
- God's Wisdom for Little Girls
- A Little Girl After God's Own Heart

Books by Jim George

- 10 Minutes to Knowing the Men and Women of the Bible
- 50 Most Important Teachings of the Bible
- The Bare Bones Bible® Handbook
- The Bare Bones Bible® Handbook for Teens
- A Boy After God's Own Heart
- A Boy's Guide to Discovering His Bible
- A Boy's Guide to Making Really Good Choices
- A Dad After God's Own Heart
- A Husband After God's Own Heart
- Know Your Bible from A to Z
- A Leader After God's Own Heart
- A Man After God's Own Heart
- A Man After God's Own Heart Devotional
- The Man Who Makes a Difference
- One-Minute Insights for Men
- A Young Man After God's Own Heart
- A Young Man's Guide to Discovering His Bible
- A Young Man's Guide to Making Right Choices

Books by Jim & Elizabeth George

- A Couple After God's Own Heart
- A Couple After God's Own Heart Interactive Workbook
- God's Wisdom for Little Boys
- A Little Boy After God's Own Heart

About the Author

Elizabeth George is a bestselling author and speaker whose passion is to teach the Bible in a way that changes women's lives. For information about Elizabeth's books or speaking ministry, to sign up for her mailings, or to share how God has used this book in your life, please contact Elizabeth at:

www.ElizabethGeorge.com